ORPHAN & MA

BODYBUI

YOGA WARRIOR

Rudy Mettia: The Jagged Road To Enlightenment

RUDY METTIA

WITH

JAN HUBBARD

www.dizzyemupublishing.com

DIZZY EMU PUBLISHING
1714 N McCadden Place, Hollywood, Los Angeles 90028
www.dizzyemupublishing.com

YOGA WARRIOR

Rudy Mettia: The Jagged Road To Enlightenment

ISBN: 978-1534755512

First published in the United States
in 2016 by Dizzy Emu Publishing

www.dizzyemupublishing.com

ORPHAN & MARINE, BOUNCER & BIKER,
BODYBUILDER & SPIRITUALIST

YOGA WARRIOR

Rudy Mettia: The Jagged Road To Enlightenment

RUDY METTIA

WITH
JAN HUBBARD

FOREWORD

I am honored to be able to write this foreword for Rudy.

Because it's a show of the respect Rudy Mettia has for me, for sure. But what it is mostly is a chance to give that respect back to Rudy.

I still remember the first day, nearly twenty years ago, when I saw Rudy in my class> He'd been dragged there by his girlfriend at the time, with her big red hair who he describes in this book. Rudy was maybe the first person to wear converse shoes without laces, which is now so trendy. I didn't know where this guy had come from but he certainly belonged in L.A. as he was most definitely a unique character.

Soon I learned one of the yoga instructors at my studio was allowing Rudy to sub her classes. Not long after that, he was asking for his own classes, all the while diligently showing up day in and day out attending other instructors' classes as well as mine.

It wasn't long before I trusted Rudy to lead my own classes as I traveled around the globe sharing the yoga I had created called *Power Yoga*. Rudy, Seane Corn and Shiva Ray were some of the very few I trusted to lead my class.

Being exposed to so many people and with so many people being exposed to Rudy, it did not take this tough, wacky, sweet, athletic man with a big heart long to win over the students and become one of Los Angeles' biggest yoga draws.

Although Rudy credits me as his major influence, he soon flew away from my nest (as a student should) and landed in many other nests, expanding his knowledge, following his intuition and developing his own unique style. Now with almost two decades experience, Rudy is shining bright with a successful training program, DVD set, online streaming service and still daily classes at my studio. This is one of the unique and special by-products of having a head full of gray hair! I got to watch the development of something as raw as Rudy was in that first class with the girl with big red hair into this yoga maestro.

One thing I really liked about this book and Rudy's story is not all that he has been through (although I was deeply touched by his story), but what he has become! To me, this book is inspirational in the sense that it expresses the fact that yoga is for everyone and, just because your past did not include peace, love and granola (mine did not either), that does not bar you from yoga wisdom. In Rudy's case, it's to the contrary - it has been his catalyst.

You definitely won't find another rough and tumble story like this in the plethora of yoga books out there and for me that is refreshing.

I can certainly recommend to you, Rudy Mettia!

Bryan Kest
Father of *Power Yoga* and founder of western based *Donation Yoga*

YOGA WARRIOR

To my beautiful daughter Scarlett Rose, you were five years old at the time I was writing this book. While you may have been a bit late getting to me in life, spiritually child, you were right on time. Your arrival changed my life for the better and in profound ways brought me full circle. Due to our late meeting in this life I may not get to spend nearly enough years with you but I trust that God has given you my warrior spirit to live fully and know that you are surrounded by love, as love is all there is. Baby, remember when you were very small and we would go out each night to search for the moon? Each night I would tell you that as long as the moon is in the sky I would always love you. Look up child, I'm here.

INTRODUCTION

If the pastel-colored buildings of Myrtle Beach were looking any more beautiful than usual in the twilight, I didn't notice. I had things on my mind, a semi-automatic tucked into the back of my pants, and a purple Crown Royal bag containing $40,000 slung over my shoulder.

Michael was already fifteen minutes late and I didn't like that. In fact, there were quite a few things I didn't like about any of this, but I needed the money badly. Besides, as Larry had assured me, it was an easy five grand.

What was I doing in Myrtle Beach on that chilly January evening in 1990 with a loaded gun and a bag full of cash? I'll get to that shortly. And who was Larry? I'll get to that too. In fact, I'll get to a lot of things, many of them not very pleasant, as I tell you about the path I have taken in life. Yoga was my eventual salvation and it took me awhile to figure it out.

Larry was probably right. Yeah, pretty soon I'd be on a plane back to L.A., wondering what I'd been so nervous about. I just had this weird feeling about things – not quite a premonition, but something slightly stronger than a hunch. And I couldn't shake it.

I'd witnessed plenty of drug deals over the past few years, of course – it would have been impossible not to have done so in my capacity as Larry's bodyguard, given he was a major league drug dealer... but this was my first time in the role as a go-between for a buyer and a seller. Maybe that's why my usual, bullet-proof self-confidence wasn't firing on all cylinders.

"Come on, motherfucker. Where are you?" I mumbled.

As if in answer, a car horn sounded a couple of short blasts. They came from a red Audi Coupe, which rolled to a stop in front of where I was stood on the sidewalk, right outside a near-empty restaurant.

"Rudy! Jump in, buddy."

I'd only met Michael once before, which happened to be on a drug deal arranged and attended by Larry. Despite what he called out through the window, I certainly didn't consider him my buddy. He was just another face among the endless faces which came and went through the revolving doors of the world Larry had introduced me to.

I got into the front seat and Michael pulled off. The first thing I noticed was that the AC was on full blast, despite the evening being fairly cool. The second thing I noticed was the sweat on Michael's forehead. Beads of it, like some kind of translucent acne.

Michael didn't apologize for being late, which pissed me off. He chose instead to make awkward attempts at chit chat in between equally awkward periods of silence. He seemed really nervous and kept fidgeting with his long greasy hair as he drove.

"We ought to be okay here," Michael said, eventually steering the Coupe into an empty parking lot behind some stores and parking it across a couple of bays. He reached under his seat and produced two kilos of cocaine from a grocery bag. They were in brick form, exactly like the cocaine you see on TV shows.

"I suppose you'll want to sample the goods?" he said, smiling nervously.

He supposed right. I loved cocaine back then, so I was familiar with how it should taste and feel, plus you don't hand over $40,000 without making sure what you're receiving is the real deal. Michael cut a hole in the middle of one of the bricks with his key without even waiting for me to answer.

I tried it and it was good.

"Are we good? We're good, right? And you got the forty?" he asked.

"Yeah, I've got it. Now, you got it," I said, handing him the Crown Royal bag. "It's all in there."

"Hey, I trust you, buddy!" he said, although he switched on the Coupe's interior light and opened the bag before conducting a fairly thorough count of the money right in front of me anyway. I kept an eye on the car park's entrance and exit until he seemed satisfied by the count.

"Great. Thanks, buddy. That's great. Thank you. You're okay to make your own way from here, right?"

Making my own way was fine by mc. My hotel was only a ten minute walk away and I was kind of anxious to be away from Michael, whose jumpy and jittery disposition seemed really odd for a guy who sold this stuff all the time.

Charles - the buyer and an *actual* buddy of mine who I knew through Larry – was waiting for me back in the hotel room when I got back.

"Everything go okay?" he asked.

"All good. Here you go," I replied, handing Charles the grocery bag with the two kilos of cocaine inside.

"Good to see you again, Rudy. Thanks for this. Have a good flight back west tomorrow and I'll see you and Larry soon."

Charles produced an envelope from his jacket pocket and handed it to me as he left. Five grand. Five grand, which in a way was Larry's way of sorting me out with a kind of severance pay. I was on my own now and I needed this money badly.

I flicked through some TV stations before deciding to get an early night. As I drifted off to sleep, I felt relieved that everything had gone okay.

Larry had been right. Easy money.

* * *

I can't even remember hearing the phone ringing but it must have done, because I was sat at the end of my hotel bed with the receiver to my ear and Charles screaming at the other end. I was still half asleep and didn't know what the hell was going on.

"What the fuck bullshit are you trying to pull? Do you think I'm fucking stupid?" Charles yelled.

The LED alarm clock on the bedside cabinet read 1.57 a.m.

"Charles, what are you talking about? It's 2 a.m."

"I don't give a fuck what time it is! These two bricks of shit you gave me aren't cocaine. Are you trying to fuck me over?"

"That's impossible. Charles, I tested it. It's coke, man."

"You'd better get your ass over here right now. Do not make me have to find you."

Something in his voice made me think that Charles having to find me would not be a good thing for me. I got dressed and made my way over to his place.

When I got there, Charles was still irate. One of the bricks of cocaine was now a big white pile on a tray in his living room. He jabbed a finger at it and told me to taste some, which I did.

"Fuck," I said, lamely.

"Damn right, fuck. That's plaster of fucking Paris."

"But... I don't understand. I tested it."

My surprise must have appeared genuine, because Charles calmed down a little and showed me what Michael had done. He had cut the hole in the middle of the brick and filled a small area with actual cocaine. The rest of the "kilo" was plaster – 2.2 pounds, to be exact. Had I been more experienced, I would have cut several holes and checked other areas of the brick, but Larry had never had a problem with Michael before, so this was a surprise.

"That son of a bitch has got my $40,000 and I don't need to plaster my fucking walls or make a fucking sculpture. You'd better hope I don't find out you're a part of this scam, Rudy."

As pissed off as Charles was, and as dangerous as I knew he could be, I didn't like the suggestion that I had played a deliberate part in ripping him off. I made the deal so I had to accept the fact that Charles getting burned was my fault, but beyond that I was as equally pissed at Michael for putting me into this situation.

"Don't be ridiculous. Why would I be here now if I was part of this and not on my way to L.A. already?"

That calmed him down but it didn't solve the problem.

I knew Michael lived in Charlotte, about a three and a half hour drive from Myrtle Beach.

"How about we catch the next flight and surprise him at his place?" I suggested.

* * *

We arrived at Michael's apartment a few hours later and parked our rental right outside before we marched up the pathway towards it. It was completely deserted.

The detective in me decided to go check out the dumpster and I started digging through the stinking trash. Sure enough, I found an envelope with Michael's name on it and the address of a post office box.

We drove on to the post office and parked on the opposite side of the street. Usually on TV shows or movies, surveillance is depicted as being exciting and edge-of-your-seat stuff. In reality, it's endless hours of boredom. All I had by way of entertainment was Charles and his non-stop whining. It was aggravating as hell, particularly after only a few hours of sleep, although by now he seemed satisfied that I wasn't part of the scam. Between the whining and the way Michael had ripped me off, I was in a real nasty mood. It was not going to be good news for Michael if he showed up.

It took over 24 hours, but Michael finally did show up. He parked his red Audi only a few meters ahead of our rental. He obviously wasn't in a state of high alert because he didn't notice me getting out of the rental, my gun in the back of my pants, following him as he sauntered into the post office.

I followed him all the way to his post office box and stood behind him. The motherfucker was actually whistling a tune as he was in the process of opening up his box!

"Hey buddy," I said through clenched teeth.

Michael stopped whistling. He turned slowly and I put the gun to his head.

I have to give him credit – he did a nice job of not shitting his pants. I had no intention of shooting him, of course. He wasn't worth life in prison. But with the gun barrel pressed against his forehead, he couldn't be sure of anything.

I grabbed his long hair and yanked him by it, practically carrying him outside to the rental car. Charles got out and sat in the back seat and I threw Michael into the passenger seat. I didn't take my gun off him for a second as I made my way into the driver's seat.

Charles had a few choice words for Michael before he got down to business.

"Where's the forty grand, you dumb piece of shit?"

"It's in the glove of my car. Please don't kill me, guys. I'm sorry, okay?"

"Sorry my ass. Hand me your goddamn keys, you sorry son of a bitch."

Michael did as he was told.

"Rudy, drive over to O'Reilly's Bar. I'll follow," said Charles, exiting the back seat.

I was glad to pull away. I don't know if anyone had noticed what was going on or not – the combination of guns and post offices usually raise an eyebrow, at least - but thankfully no cops came.

When I looked in the rear view mirror, Charles was holding up the Crown Royal bag out the window to show me he had the money.

We arrived at O'Reilly's Bar soon after. Michael's friend owned it and since it was the middle of the afternoon, no one was there. We took a corner booth that was out of the way, just in case anyone dropped by and wondered what was going on, and Charles counted the money right there on the table while Michael fidgeted with his lank hair.

"It's ten grand short, you fucking miserable cocksucker," Charles spat.

I pushed the gun into Michael's ribs. He squirmed and wriggled as we threatened him with various forms of medieval torture. By now I could see in his eyes that he was terrified of me. Ripping me off had made him nervous, but seeing how angry he had caused me to get now inspired a genuine fear in him.

"Bubba has it, guys. Please can we all just relax? You'll get it all back, okay? I'm sorry!"

I knew Bubba, again through Larry. He lived in Greenville, South Carolina, which was about two hours away. We didn't particularly want to have to bring Michael along with us for the drive, but we couldn't risk him calling Bubba and warning him we were on our way, so Charles threw a few dollars at his bar manager friend and he agreed to keep Michael incommunicado for a while.

We made the usual two-hour drive in a little over an hour and easily found Bubba, standing next to his car with his girlfriend in it. I'm sure she was horrified when I shoved the business end of my .45 into Bubba's ribcage and made the same threats I'd made earlier to Michael.

"Rudy, man, I didn't know it was you he was ripping off! Honestly, man! If I did..."

"Shut the fuck up, Bubba. Just hand over the ten grand."

Bubba quickly gave us the cash, saving his own butt, but he'd already spent $5,000. So we were five grand short.

Charles had $35,000 of his $40,000 back, and having seen me in action, he figured I deserved the $5,000 he'd already paid me, busted deal or not. So he let me keep it.

Before we parted ways and I got a taxi to go to the airport, Charles told me he never wanted to see me again. That was fine with me. I got on a plane to California and that officially marked the end of my venture into drug deals.

* * *

Let's take things back just a little bit.

Enlightenment is something I began chasing under circumstances that might be considered unusual. During my brief tenure as a policeman, my best friend was a charismatic drug dealer named Larry. It's not often you see cops who are mesmerized in such a positive way by a criminal, but in the 26 years I had lived at the time, he was absolutely the coolest guy I'd ever met. He had a flashy ride, a Harley-Davidson motorcycle and a speed boat. He also had a colorful past.

When he was in the Marines, he began selling drugs and apparently didn't do it very carefully because he got caught. The Marines tend to frown on such exercises, so they whacked Larry with a dishonorable discharge, which didn't seem to bother him.

If Larry had been born a century earlier during the days of the Wild Wild West, he would have been an outlaw, but a celebrated one . . . someone like Butch Cassidy. He had a small armory of military weapons that he was not opposed to using. His guard dogs were, of course, pit bulls, but they were a spectacular snow white. Larry was fearless, had a magnetic personality, told many tall tales that fascinated a crowd of followers who partied with us during long, cocaine-fueled nights and was a big influence on me.

In 1986, I had known Larry for several months and although he lived a daily life of danger, he was pretty carefree. He also was the kind of a guy who did things on a whim and some of that rubbed off on me – for example, when he suggested I leave the police department to work and hang with him. Strangely enough, at the time, it seemed to make perfect sense. So I agreed instantly, left law enforcement and became Larry's bodyguard and partner in crime.

One day, he said he had broken up with his girlfriend and was very upset about it so he announced, without any warning, that he was leaving Myrtle Beach, South Carolina, where we were living and working at the time.

"I'm getting the hell out of here and moving to California," he said, and then asked a question that would change my life: "You want to go?"

Before I could answer, he said "I've got some cash so why don't you ride shotgun with me and I'll give you $5,000? We'll figure out how to make money once we get out there."

After that, I'm guessing it took between five and six seconds for me to say "yes." I had always wanted to move to California but I thought there'd be a little more planning involved. The adventure appealed to me, however. I pictured myself as a modern-day Jack Kerouac and this was going to be a game-changing experience.

In keeping with the impulsiveness of the trip, when we crossed the state line entering California, I decided that since I was starting a new life, I needed a new identity. For 29 years, I had been known as Gary Smith. But "Gary Smith" did not reflect the daring, the glamour or the uniqueness of what I was doing. So I decided to part ways with Gary.

We were headed for Hollywood, so I thought of something theatrical, maybe use one name. What about Quest? Yes. Very dramatic and wasn't that exactly what I was on? A quest? If Prince Rogers Nelson could be known as Prince, why not one name for me? I also considered Masco – short for masculine. Sounds silly now, but then who thought Kramer would become a memorable TV character?

After jettisoning those names, I began to seriously think about whom I wanted to be and I was motivated by something that had lasted too few years – my family. I decided to pay tribute to the father I never knew and took Rudy, his first name, which also happened to be my middle name. And to my Italian mother who I knew far too briefly, I took her maiden name, Mettia. Or so I thought. I later discovered I had misspelled the last name. It should have been "Mattia." But I made the decision under the heavy influence of Jack Daniels while hurtling across the California border on I-10 in a 1979 GMC Jimmy at midnight. So I had no handy access to the family tree for the correct spelling.

It may be surprising to longtime friends, but I never legally changed my name. On my taxes, driver's license and other important documents, I'm still Gary Smith. But Gary's been gone half my life now and I'm glad for that, not because of the name, but because life has been much better for Rudy than it was for Gary. The irony, however, is that some of the horrific situations Gary encountered and ultimately survived went a long way towards making Rudy successful.

I look at my life as a trip from circumstance to vision. You go from a circumstance, in my case as someone who spent most of his formative years with no close family or meaningful role models, and you can either be enslaved by it or you can rise out. I wasn't purposely rising out of it when I began succeeding in life as a member of the Marines, but for the first time in my life, I was free.

And that's how I spent many years of my adult life - as a man who was free to make any decision he wanted to make. Some of them were great. Some were weird. Some were dangerous. Some were laughable. All, as you will see, are memorable.

The most important result for me, however, was the jagged road I traveled led me to the focus, the discipline and the tranquility of yoga. Until I passed my 40th birthday, there was turbulence in my life - some of it caused by others; much of it caused by the choices I made. I had major anger issues for many years and resolving those was a complicated process. Even as I pursued a life of yoga in morning classes, at night my job as a nightclub bouncer led to regular physical violence. So I'd beat the hell out of people at night and the next morning I would embrace the tranquility of yoga. As I often told friends at the time, I had one foot in the dark and one foot in the light.

Ultimately, I completed the transition and it certainly is a lot easier on the body. More importantly, however, is that yoga has given me laser-like clarity in a unique way. I had already found a source of enlightenment in weight training. For 15 years before I discovered yoga, I was a dedicated bodybuilder. It was my wellspring, my rock when I needed to get grounded and a place where I flourished. In fact, it was how I discovered yoga - a story you will read in this book.

For me, yoga was an extension of bodybuilding. It gave me the opportunity to do with my mind what I had done with my body. It turned me introspective and enabled me to develop my Yoga Warrior philosophy, which I teach in my classes and practice in my everyday life. All great warrior traditions from the Samurai to the Sioux to the mythical Amazon women warriors have a cause. Ours is a battle for the liberation of our minds – the constant struggle to overcome weakness, a lack of discipline, fear, laziness, ignorance, cowardice, envy, greed and all vices rooted in ego. Our minds and bodies are our weapons and we can use the inspiration of our *Asanas* and the power of our will to purify and cleanse them.

I won my battle but there were mighty challenges along the way and there were times when I had to overcome my most formidable enemy, who was me. In my story, there are bits of tragedy, fear, humor, discovery, accomplishment, stupidity, danger, violence, daring, celebrity, success and, finally, spirituality and peace. As I look back, it was a hard road to enlightenment. But it was never boring.

CHAPTER 1 - MOM IS WHAT?

Yoga first entered my life when I was nine years old, although I did not discover that for several decades. When I look back at my state of consciousness on that life-changing spring day in 1970, I know the calmness I felt was similar to what I would eventually teach in my yoga classes. It wasn't something I was striving for and it certainly wasn't as pleasant. But it was there.

I wasn't old enough to understand the turmoil I would encounter as a result of the family problem we had that day. I could not see that I would soon be leaving the only home I'd ever known and be moving to several homes, many of which I would never remember. I could not grasp that, in a short time, I would never again live with a parent or sibling. But even though I do not have a vivid memory of exactly how I felt, when the news was delivered, I must have known I was fucked.

There were three children in my family. Freddy was 12 years older than me but had a different father. Caresse, my sister, was three years older than me and went by the name of Chris.

As the oldest, Freddy was in charge and that was scary. Freddy had a temper that would frighten a pit bull and a demeanor that was ornery on a good day. He was in the Army at the time, stationed in Vietnam, and the war had done nothing to make him a more pleasant person.

Because of our family emergency, he was allowed to come to our home in Greensboro, North Carolina, and he was the one who delivered the bad news. My sister and I were sitting silently on the sofa, not quite sure what was going to happen. But it had been a while since our mother had been home, so we were hoping to get some good news.

Freddy entered the room with the ever-present scowl on his slender bony face and started to speak. When I picture it now, it is in slow motion and he mutters the words like his mouth is full of molasses.

"I . . . have . . . bad . . . news. . . . Mother . . . has . . . died. . . . She . . . won't . . . be . . . coming . . . home."

Chris immediately began wailing, fell to the floor and was shaking violently, but I just sat there motionless, emotionless and silent. I'm sure I was shocked but I did not cry and not because I didn't love my mother. I did then and I still do now. In fact, when I began recording my thoughts for this book, I cried the first time I talked about that day.

Looking back, however, I might have been in the midst of my first experience with *Pranayama* breathing. *Pranayama* is a Sanskrit word meaning "extension of the *prāṇa*, or "breath" or "extension of the life force." Unknowingly at nine years old, I might have found that breathing in a deep and controlled way allowed me to relax during a very intense time. *Pranayama* breathing would be a recurring force in my life and, eventually, a fundamental part of my yoga teaching philosophy. When I revert to my southern drawl and ask students, "Y'all breathing?" they are humored by it. I think on the day of my mother's death, I somehow found a way to breathe.

I'm sure I grieved eventually but like some periods of my early life, I have blocked out many of the memories. Unfortunately at that time, I was prepared for losing a parent because one of the first pieces of information I remember receiving in my life was that my father had died when I was six months old. I can't remember who told me the story, but it had to have been my mother. He had a heart defect and doctors told him the condition would end his life at some point. He might be 25, 35 or 55, but his heart would at some point stop working. That prognosis proved correct when he was 33.

In my yoga classes, part of my physical approach to teaching is centered on six actions when performing a posture. The actions also apply when I consider choices in my life in yoga *Asanas*. I first organize, stabilize and analyze the posture. Then the work shifts and becomes mental as I observe and then adjust, either physically or mentally, depending on the circumstances. Finally, I reflect back on the end result.

When I apply that to my state of mind when my mom died, I can speculate – because I have only a few hazy memories – that my mind must have organized the information, analyzed and stabilized it. She had already been in the hospital, so I knew she was not well. I had no choice but to observe the scene that I was in the middle of, and I'm sure I had an instinctive feeling that adjustments would be forthcoming. And it is certainly easy for me to see now that I was already reflecting back on my short time with my mother and sensing the forthcoming challenges that were drifting my way, as dark as southern storm clouds.

My point is that even though it took many years to come to this revelation, my life has always been connected to yoga. I think that is how I survived the death of both parents, too many foster homes to remember – including several years of living and working on a pig farm – the Marines, two thankfully unsuccessful court martials, many years as a bouncer and doorman for bars ranging from seedy to chic, several years working as a body guard for individuals who ranged from a drug dealer to Elizabeth Taylor and finally, rewardingly, as a dedicated yoga instructor devoted to innovation and enlightenment.

* * *

I have this beautiful portrait of my mother, whose name was Vera, that I have always had hanging on a wall in places where I lived. At the bottom of it is an inscription that reads: "Bari, 1946." Bari is an Eastern Italy port city on the Adriatic Sea and is the resting place for the relics of St. Nicholas, a fourth-century saint who had a reputation not only as a miracle worker, but also as a generous and prolific gift-giver. You know him as St. Nick, the inspiration for Santa Claus. Maybe he's the reason why my mother went overboard every Christmas with an artificial white Christmas tree, red ornaments and green decorations, colors that happen to grace the Italian flag.

My mom came to the U.S. in 1946 thanks to her first

husband, Clayton Gray, Freddy's father. Mom was tiny, about 5'2" on a good day. Clayton 'towered' over her at 5'8".

The first memory I have of Clayton was the day of my mother's funeral. He drove with us in the big black town car the funeral home provided to take the family to Forrest Lawn cemetery, where she was buried. My dad is not far away, at rest on the military side of the property. His grave is marked by a simple white cross.

The gate where we first tried to enter was closed and I remember Freddy, being Freddy, was yelling, cursing and generally raising hell because, of course, it should have been opened for him. I half expected him to tear the gate down, but he didn't. There was no one around to open it for us, which caused a funeral procession traffic jam so everyone had to back up to go another way around.

I would not see Clayton again until he was nearly 90 years old and it was great to visit with him because even at that age, he was spry and a colorful story teller and he told me many stories about my mother.

They had met when Clayton was in the Army and stationed in Bari during World War II, which was in the control of the Allies. At the time, half the village was controlled by the British and the other half by the Americans.

One day, a British officer approached Clayton, who was in charge of a crew building an officers' club, and asked if he had any jobs for some of the locals.

"I'm up to my neck in Italians," said Clayton.

"This particular local is a pretty little blonde," the Brit

responded. "She's 18 years old and really needs a job."

Clayton was, as he should have been, intrigued.

So he met my mother and was immediately attracted to her. A year later, they had Freddy. When it was time for Clayton to go home, however, my mother couldn't go with him because she was not a U.S. citizen. They had to get married for her to legally enter America and there was a complication because she was a staunch Catholic. Clayton wasn't. At the time, non-Catholics could not get married in the church, but my mom refused to get married anywhere else.

Even though I do not have Clayton's genes, his solution to the problem would be the sort of decision I would later make in the Marines. He decided that it made perfect sense to steal a jeep, which he then drove 300 miles to Rome. His plan was to infiltrate the Vatican and find someone who had the authority to allow a protestant to be married in the church. Amazingly, that's exactly what he did. Clayton managed to get his application for a waiver approved. He even had it stamped with an official signature stamp that said: "Pope Pius XII."

According to Clayton, it wasn't unusual for the church to grant such easy approval because after World War II, there were big economic problems and a shortage of jobs in Italy. So if the church could get some of the young women married and allow them to have a better life, they did.

Around that time, Vera had the portrait painted and brought it with her to the U.S. I learned a little more about it because while I was talking to Clayton and asking him questions, he pulled out an old shoebox from beneath his bed and produced a photo of the same portrait. Clayton stared at the photo for a long second and with a faint tear in his eye said, “Son, I never remarried because I always loved your mother. I still do.”

We sat there together in silence with his thumb and forefinger holding one corner of the photo and mine holding onto the other, Clayton and I holding on for the same reason, for the love we both felt for a woman who left us too soon.

The wooden frame is the original one, so it is now 70 years old. I told Clayton I always wanted to change it. But Clayton told me to leave the frame on because of its historical value. It turns out that in the POW camp, there were some Nazi soldiers and Clayton had found out that one of them was a carpenter. So Clayton ordered the guy to build the frame. That’s pretty unique. I kind of look at it as a symbol of our superiority over the Nazis. I don’t imagine that before the war, the carpenter thought he’d be an inmate working for a love sick American. But that’s what happened and the proof still hangs on my wall.

* * *

Clayton and my mom left Italy as Mr. and Mrs. Gray. Clayton left the military and they moved into the Adirondacks in upstate New York. I have a picture of my mom posing in a one piece swimsuit, standing by a lake and looking very much like Betty Gable.

They were happy for a while, but jobs were scarce and when he could not find steady work, Clayton went back into the military. My mother stayed with his parents, but they weren't as nice as Clayton. They were wealthy and looked down on her because they considered her an Italian peasant. She had friends who had settled in North Carolina and when she could no longer tolerate the disdain of Clayton's parents, she moved south. Unfortunately for Clayton, his parents' disrespect resulted in him losing a wife. Shortly after she arrived in North Carolina, she met Rudy David Smith, my father, who promptly stole her from Clayton.

Oddly, all I know about my dad came from Freddy, who had moved away from New York with my mom and was living with her when she met my dad. When I was about 20, I went to a bar and had a beer with Freddy and found out that much of my aggressive temperament (my drill instructor would refer to it as my "killer instinct") came from my dad.

"You know, your father used to drink in this place," Freddy told me. "If he had a few too many, he would get in fights and empty this joint."

That would at least partially explain my love of fighting that developed in the Marines and continued for many years afterward. Freddy described my dad as a drinker, brawler, cigarette-smoking type of a guy. He was of Scottish-Irish descent and he fit the stereotype – tough, loud and rowdy. If you were fool enough to offend him, you had a fight on your hands with a 6-foot-1 bruiser.

My dad was the spitting image of Robert F. Kennedy and I

would guess he was quite the ladies' man. My mom obviously wanted to be with him very much because she got a divorce from Clayton. That had to be difficult for her because the Catholic Church did not allow or recognize divorces. But you could get a civil divorce, which is obviously what she did. She then married my dad and they had my sister and me.

By the time I was old enough to begin building memories, my mom was very Americanized. There's a picture of her waiving a tiny American flag that they give you when you pledge allegiance and become a tax-paying citizen. I never thought we had anything more than a lower middle class existence, but looking back now I guess we did all right. Mom owned a small Italian restaurant and she drove a Cadillac, so we were at least comfortable. When I turned 18, I received $4,000 from social security and I'm sure she wouldn't be pleased to know I spent all of it on a sports car. Or maybe she would.

I do know that my mom had five passions:

1. Elvis Presley
2. Tom Jones
3. Dean Smith
4. Charlie Scott
5. Italian opera

Elvis was by far her favorite. She played his records constantly and whenever one of his movies was on, she was glued to the TV set. I remember *Love Me Tender* playing and Elvis getting shot and laying in the grass dying near the end of the movie and my mother crying like it really happened.

She also loved Tom Jones, the singer, but not as much as Elvis. Jones was in his 20s at the time and he had learned from Elvis how to grind his hips. He wore tight pants, shirts buttoned halfway up and he aggressively flirted with women in the audience. When he began performing in Las Vegas, women would throw their hotel keys on the stage. He was good looking, talented and sexy. Women loved him and my mom was one of them. The funny thing is in 1993, I threw a party at the Viper Room in West Hollywood and about 300 people came. Tom Jones was one of them. I'm sure my mother would have been thrilled if she knew I met him and told him how much she loved him.

Basketball played a big part of my youth and one reason was that North Carolina's legendary coach Dean Smith used to eat at my mother's restaurant. Smith's teams won almost 900 games during his career and the Tar Heels won two national championships, although both happened after my mother died. Coach Smith made the program a great one and my mother was thrilled when he came to eat at her place.

My mom had put up a basketball goal in the back of the restaurant. I used to practice on it after school as I waited for her to close up. One day, as the sun shone down on me and my long shadow, she came out of the back door. She was smiling ear to ear and proudly introduced me to coach Smith. I think she almost fainted when coach started to teach me the finer points of free throw shooting.

To this day I never miss a UNC game and when we win big games I always shed a tear thinking of how my mother lived and died with each game. Coach Smith to this day remains one of my biggest influences.

Charlie Scott was the first African-American to be given a scholarship at North Carolina and was a great player. He eventually played 10 years as a pro, was on three NBA All-Star teams and was the third leading scorer on the 1976 Boston Celtics team that won the NBA championship. My mom really didn't know much about basketball, coming from Italy, but whenever the Tar Heels were on TV, she'd watch them, hollering happily when they won and crying when they lost. We had a basket in our back yard and my mother would send me out there as soon as I got home from school. "If you are going to be as good as Charlie Scott," she said, "you have to practice." I was the only kid that had to practice basketball before I did my homework.

The one pleasure my mom brought with her from Italy was a love of Italian opera. And maybe it was that part of her brain that also created the elegant name of Caresse for my sister. It's kind of funny to think back to my mom listening to one record by Elvis, the next by Tom Jones and then an Italian opera. The woman definitely had diverse tastes.

Apart from his passing away, if my mom told me stories about my dad, I don't remember them. And because I was so young when she died, I have far too few memories of her. But I am thankful for the ones I have. Remembering how happy Elvis, Tom and North Carolina basketball made her always makes me smile. I also have a powerful memory of the way she smelled, so vivid that when I was in my late 30s and taking acting classes in Los Angeles, I wrote a story about the scent of my mother and how I used to sleep with my head on her lap. That was an exercise designed to stimulate creativity and when I decided to write about her, the memories came flooding back. She was a small lady with blonde hair and I just remember her passion – so joyous about things she loved and so emotional when things went bad, like Elvis getting shot in that movie. But I guess that should not be surprising. That passion was part of her Italian heritage.

* * *

The memory of the last time I saw my mom is vivid. We lived on a corner lot and one day I came home from school and entered the house, but it was empty. I went into the back yard and over the fence I could see her white Cadillac parked out on the side street, but I couldn't see her in it. I knew she had to be around somewhere.

I had looked everywhere so the only option left was to open the car door, which I did, and found a scary sight.

She was lying in the back seat and had a confused look on her face. She tried to talk, but couldn't. Her eyes were crossed and rolled back into her head. At that point, I went blank. I don't remember who I went to for help, or if an ambulance came, or even how long it was between that moment and Freddy telling us that she had died.

We later found out that she had an aneurism. Because she was in such bad shape, my sister and I were not allowed to visit her in the hospital. I do remember being very angry about that.

My final contact with her was that moment in the back seat of that Cadillac. Anyone who loses their mother at age nine is going to have their life impacted negatively. If it is a single mother, the effect is multiplied many times. And if there are no other family members willing or able to provide a home for two devastated grade-school aged kids, life becomes a nightmare.

CHAPTER 2 - PTSD PARENTING

When my mother had the aneurism, my brother Freddy was serving as an Army gunner on a riverboat in Vietnam. He was allowed to come home to take care of us and did such a bang-up job that my sister and I were soon wards of the great state of North Carolina and sent to foster care.

In fairness to him, no one should be subjected to the terror that was part of his everyday life. Each morning that he woke up in the jungles of Vietnam, he knew that day could be his last. Since he didn't have the sunniest of dispositions anyway, life in hell did not improve his temperament. So in a matter of days, he went from wielding an M-60 machine gun and laying down suppressive fire on Charlie to parenting kids aged 12 and nine. Since that was not part of the training in Army infantry school, he was in way over his head.

Only 21 years old, Freddy was not much more than a kid himself and his life had slapped him around a few times. He'd had to endure the pain of his mom divorcing his dad. At age 12, his stepfather died. And now his mother had died in a very disturbing way. Add in the war and I'm convinced that Freddy had Post Traumatic Stress Disorder (PTSD), a condition that at the time would not be recognized for another 10 years.

In short, he was a certified nut job. Still is, I'm glad to report.

I have few specific memories of those times. There was nothing pleasant to remember. It would have been nice to shoot baskets with my big brother in the back yard. It would be great to remember family gatherings at night - dinner, board games, TV shows. Instead, Freddy imagined himself as a drill instructor and he tried to discipline me like I was a recruit in boot camp. He even had me spit shine his boots, and it was that task that eventually sent my sister and me out of the house.

After I'd spent a stupid amount of time on them one day, Freddy came into the living room to inspect my work. Picking up one of the boots, he took a cursory look at it before letting it drop to the ground.

"These goddamn boots look like polished shit!" he screamed.

My mouth, already dry from a long shift of producing saliva-polish, went even dryer. It wasn't just the screaming – Freddy had a dangerous look in his eye, which I was starting to know all too well. Despite this, or maybe because of it, I felt the need to defend my hard work.

"Well, Freddy, if you had a good rag, I bet I could shine them better."

If I'd hoped to calm Freddy down, I failed.

Unbeknownst to me at the time, when you were in the military and you said "you," the sergeant or officer would say "Ewe? What? Are you some kind of female sheep? That's what ewe is." So when I said "you," I meant it in the most general terms but, lacking originality or common sense (I was nine fucking years old), Freddy screamed "Ewe? I'm no goddamn female sheep!"

Freddy wasn't good at many things, but he was very

accomplished at making himself angry about nothing. So since he was in a rage about shoe polish, I decided the best thing to do was to get the hell away from him for as long as it took for him to simmer down.

I took off running, dodging past him and flying out of the living room, through the hall and out into the street. I could hear him bearing down on me and I dug as deep as I could to just keep on running.

The whack came down on the back of my head. Hard. It knocked me off balance and I fell down, my face slamming against the concrete before I could even raise my hands to help spread the impact.

I lay there, stunned. My eyes were blurry with tears and dancing stars, but I could see Freddy's shadow looming over me on the sidewalk.

"Fucking ewe," he mumbled.

To my relief, his shadow turned and moved away, back towards the house.

I just lay there for a while, out on the street. A quick exploratory movement of my tongue revealed that I had chipped a tooth, and it's a chip that I still sport today. Eventually I picked myself up and went back into the house. Where else was there for me to go?

The incident wasn't unusual. He smacked us around because he was too young, too dumb and too violent to ever learn parenting skills.

A few days later, Chris and I were sat in the living room and there was a knock at the front door. We could hear Freddy walking down the hall from the kitchen to go and see who was there. I couldn't hear all of what was being said, but I could hear a different tone in Freddy's voice to the usual one we were used to. He sounded respectful, maybe even a little scared, and he was finishing every short sentence with the word 'sir.'

Freddy entered the living room, followed by a couple of uniformed cops. Compared to Freddy, who I thought of as old, these two big guys looked ancient, although both of them were probably only in their early thirties.

Freddy looked down at the ground as he spoke to us.

"The officers want to speak to you both."

Clearly Freddy's abusive ways must have gotten around the neighborhood and someone – a concerned neighbor, most likely – had reported him to the authorities.

Chris and I were separated into different rooms and one of the cops asked me a bunch of questions. They started off fairly innocuous – How was school? What sports did I like? Those sorts of things. But they became more and more focused on home life.

"Does your brother hit you and your sister, son?"

Some kind of family loyalty kicked in because I tried to cover for Freddy when I gave my answer. That's what kids do for guardians. But my youthful innocence betrayed him because when I denied that he beat us, I said, "He doesn't beat us any more than other parents beat their kids."

Maybe I wasn't just trying to convince the cop that this was true. Maybe I was trying to convince myself.

Whether it was the neighbor's report, our individual answers to the cops' questions – hell, maybe even my chipped tooth, which I'm sure the officers noticed - that was it for Freddy. Chris and I were removed from our home and since we knew of no family anywhere close, we went into foster care.

I did not see Freddy again for 12 years

When I did finally see him again, I was three years into my Marine Corps tour of duty, 21 years old, 6-foot-1 inches tall and weighed a rock solid 230 pounds. I towered over Freddy, who had Clayton's genetic makeup, which made him about 100 pounds lighter than me. I don't know if Freddy flashed back to the shoe incident, but I did. And although I had moved past any negative feelings long before, I did allow myself the luxury of thinking: "Little man, you want to try and whack me again? Bring it on."

By that time, however, I had been through so much that revenge for the chipped tooth was the last thing on my mind. And in the big picture, as weird as this may seem as we move forward with my life story – especially after I introduce you to the Pughs – being taken from the home began the process of making me who I am today. I can look back at my life and realize that each and every experience contributed to my growth as a person. I can honestly say I would not change one thing that happened to me in my life.

* * *

Other than a few instances, I have blocked out that period of my life. For two years, I was in several foster homes and I was in such a daze that I don't remember how many. Some families volunteer for emergency foster care and kids spend one night with them. Some are for several days.

I do remember a little about the first foster home, but there is a reason for that. The mom's name was Laura and I'm guessing that my behavior must have been a bit disruptive. When you agree to be an emergency foster home, you don't get a well-adjusted kid, you get a time bomb. It became apparent that although Laura was open to offering a permanent home, the offer didn't extend to me.

One night, I left my room to use the bathroom and I could hear Laura talking to the social services worker. Talk about timing. I very clearly heard Laura say to the social worker "I can keep the girl, but that boy has to go."

I was still angry about losing my mom, but my world was so empty then that I don't remember being sad or hurt by that. In fact, I don't think I gave a damn and I must have expected it. Since my mom had died, I was living in the moment and thought nothing about the next hour, the next day, the next month or the next house I was going to live in. I could imagine only the present.

The reason I remember Laura is that when I left, my sister stayed. And this is where the foster system fails. I did not see Chris or have any communication with her again until I was 18. Chris stayed with Laura all the way through high school and college and they are still close to this day. You would think that somewhere along the way, Laura or families I lived with would have been sensitive to what happened to us. We had lost both parents and been removed from my brother's care because of abuse. Neither of us left the greater Greensboro area, but neither Laura nor any of the families I stayed with had Chris and I write each other, call on the phone or even make occasional visits.

When I look back, however, I realize that I lived in houses, not homes. I was a visitor, not a family member. Some foster homes welcome orphans into their families. Others provide an important social service by giving abandoned kids a place to sleep and food to eat, but they draw family lines that are not crossed. And others do it for the government stipends they get for giving kids a place to sleep and live – and also for the cheap labor. Actually the term "slave labor" is more accurate in my experiences.

Greensboro was a city of about 150,000 that was surrounded by a bunch of farming communities and I ended up on a couple of them. At the first one, I was a little like a stray dog. The family, whose names I do not remember, would take their biological kids to the pool, to movies, and leave me behind like I was a pet. They did try to keep me busy, leaving me with a list of chores to accomplish – picking tomatoes, watermelons, tending to the chickens. But I was not included in anything that was fun.

Overall, during that period, it was the *Lord of the Flies*. I was on my own and must have not been very successful at it because I don't remember staying there very long. My one vivid memory is the wildlife. I remember hearing the screaming of rabbits in the forest. I followed the sound by ear and eventually found a rabbit being squeezed to death by a big black snake. I decided to intervene, grabbed a club and beat them both to death. It scared the hell out of me but I figured the rabbit need some relief.

I also witnessed a giant Red-tailed Hawk sweep down from the sky, scoop up a hen in the barnyard, carry her to the top of a tree and devour her. It just so happens that the hawk is my totem; the symbol that represents my past.

* * *

I had long-term stays in two foster homes and they were headed by men as different as Rush Limbaugh and Homer Simpson. The first one was the Pughs, who rejected going to church as a Sunday experience because for them, it was a daily obligation. They were so fire-and-brimstone that if they were in a thesaurus, they'd be a synonym for Southern Baptist Rednecks. The Pughs did provide a wonderful service to society by housing, by their count, 435 orphans for varying lengths of time over 30 years. It was their passion, but there was also a practical side to it:

Cheap labor.

If you lived with the Pughs, they worked your ass off. I was there from ages 13 to 16 and every summer I worked in a tobacco field from dawn until dark. They were contracted by a family nearby that owned a tobacco plantation, which seemed to be the size of a small country. There were rows and rows of tobacco, stretching out as far as the eye could see, an endless forest of 10-foot tall plants that consumed us for most of the summer. The Pughs were not the type to vacation at the beach.

When you harvest tobacco, the top leaves are harvested last. You start with the leaves that are buried in the ground. There are like four leaves in the ground and then the stalk has about 10 more rows of leaves. You stack the leaves under your arm until you get enough to where you take them to a tractor on the road. The reason to start at dawn is the stifling Carolina heat in July through September. At the end of the day, you hang the leaves upside down in barns to cure the tobacco. The work was backbreaking - for me, the most grueling in my life. And I was a teenager.

But I took great pride in doing it and to this day, part of my work ethic is from working in those fields. I don't remember dreading it at all. Everyone had to do it, so there was no room for, and no tolerance of, complaining. If you could handle your share of the work without whining, you were better than the others. I think that fueled my competitiveness, which is character strength for me. Plus, when I think back to it, being in the fields, overheated and exhausted, enabled me to forget my circumstances. I didn't have to think about not having a mother, father, sister, brother. I just had to work.

* * *

Although the Pughs worked the tobacco plantation to supplement their income, they did not spend extra money on items they considered incidental – like food for the kids. The primary business of their farm was raising pigs and you could imagine what a joy it was working with those lovely-smelling animals. My gift from that experience was worms in my stools and ringworms in my legs.

It was apparent that the Pughs didn't have a lot of money, and I'm sure that was one reason they had so many foster kids. It was cheap labor for their farm work and they could provide a large crew for their summer tobacco job while also getting stipends from the state.

But the food. Oh my God. I'm sure they serve a higher quality in homeless shelters. The Pughs had found a way to keep costs down. At the end of each day they would go to a market nearby and get loads of sweets, donuts and apple pies from the bakery. I don't know if they got them free or paid a small fee because those were the leftovers not to be sold to the public but tossed in the landfill. But I do know they were a regular part of our diet.

They at least picked out the best stuff for us kids before giving the rest to the pigs. But despite the intake of millions of calories and gallons of sugar, the result of the hard work and inadequate diet was malnourishment. When I left that farm before my sophomore year in high school, I weighed 120 pounds with legs and arms like twigs.

Life with the Pughs offered plenty of work, but little in the way of nutrition, leisure or social activities with one exception. I had inherited a shotgun, a .22 bolt action rifle and a pearl handle pocket knife with a thin six-inch blade from my grandfather. I was allowed to go into the woods to shoot and hunt, but it became obvious that I should not have been allowed to have the knife.

One day I was entertaining friends with my knife skills and I managed to plunge the entire four-inch blade into my thigh. Fearing I would be in a world of shit if the Pughs found out, I pulled the blade from my leg and placed two band-aids on the wound. I figured the Pughs would never be the wiser, but when I walked into the house, Mrs. Pugh screamed bloody murder. I looked down and blood was trickling down my leg and my foot was covered with it. I've always had a high threshold for pain. That was the day I discovered it.

Kenneth Pugh was a deacon in the church, a quiet, good-hearted religious man. He also had a dark sense of humor. One of the "privileges" I had involved a new-born piglet, which I named Pug. I raised him from birth and eventually he weighed about 600 pounds. On one cold frost bitten winter morning, Pugh took me outside and told me to call Pug, who had grown and was now my pet hog.

I didn't know what he wanted Pug for, but Pug would always come when I called him so I started yelling out.

"Sooey, sooey, sooey! Come on, Pug!"

I hadn't really paid attention to the .22 rifle Pugh had because it wasn't uncommon to carry rifles around the farm. Sure enough, Pug emerged and trotted over towards me and Pugh. I guess he was expecting a scrap of food. What neither Pug nor I was expecting was for Pugh to point the gun between Pug's eyes and shoot him, which was exactly what he did. He then produced a knife and cut Pug's throat. Blood came gushing out, spewing hot steam in the frigid morning air.

I was stunned. All I could think was "Son-of-a-bitch, my pig is dead."

They hung Pug upside down from a tree to drain his blood, then they placed him in a giant tub of boiling water so they could scrape all his hair off and gut him. It was a gruesome sight.

But throughout the winter, the ham and bacon we were able to eat eased my pain at losing Pug. He tasted a hell of a lot better than the sugary, crappy sweets so ultimately, I was proud. I had raised a very tasty pig.

Since I had to work so hard on the farm and I was so young, I learned quickly and became a good farmer and in one case, a good rancher/veterinarian. One day I was looking for our pony, which was named Dolly. The Pughs had a large property, about 20 acres, and I found her lying down near the end of the edge of the farm. I quickly became aware that she was in labor because a colt began coming out of her. So I jumped in and with both hands assisted her with the birth. Unfortunately, the colt was stillborn, but it was a moving experience that I remember vividly.

* * *

The brutality of shooting a pig in front of horrified teenager was entertaining to Pugh, but he considered activities like dancing, music and movies unsavory. They were forbidden except, of course, for gospel music in church.

TV was mostly tame at the time, but shows like *All in the Family* were breaking ground with episodes about issues like homosexuality, rape, religion, abortion, menopause, and impotence. Looking back, I can understand not being allowed to watch that in a religious household. But *The Brady Bunch*? *Partridge Family*? *Wonderful World of Disney*? They were not allowed. The only shows we could watch were *Gunsmoke* and professional wrestling. I could see Marshal Dillon serving as a role model. But Killer Kowalski and Andre the Giant?

Even *Monday Night Football* was off limits, which eventually worked in my favor. When I was about to turn 16 and enter my sophomore year in high school, I really wanted more of a social life with other kids. I had become a little defiant towards the Pughs - obviously, I was a teenager. I don't know how rebellious I could be because they were so strict and there was nothing a foster kid could really do, but I was at that age where you don't shut your mouth. I kept griping about not being able to play sports and have a better life. I don't remember if I complained to social services or if the Pughs told them, but it became evident that I had to move.

The next place was only five miles down the road, but it might as well have been in another solar system. I was allowed to move and I soon discovered the Pughs' way of life was not the standard. During the three years I lived with them, one of the biggest scandals they told us about involved a neighbor down the road who drank beer. I actually believed that if the guy was not the devil, he was a close relative. When I left the Pughs to move in with another family, it took about 30 seconds to discover how wrong that was.

* * *

"Boy, you got a goddamn driver's license?" were the first words out of Bill Stein's mouth. Not "Hello" or "Nice to meet you" or "How you doing?" I was stunned because even though I had heard the word before, I'd never heard it at home during my three years in the Pughs' house.

Bill Stein was a wild-looking character. He had long hair, a full beard and bore a remarkable resemblance to Waylon Jennings. He was head of my new foster family and my first impression was pure fear. Was a driver's license required to live there? I had no desire to go back to the pig farm.

"No sir," I said, quivering slightly. "I don't have a license."

"Well that's a bitch," he said, "because that means you're going to have to walk to the store to get me some beer."

Suddenly, I had a feeling that I had not had since before my mother died. I remember my first thought vividly:

"This is going to be a lot of fun."

And it was. Bill Stein made sure I had a driver's license so I could begin running his errands – more specifically his beer errands. In no time, I had an after-school job and bought a car – a

1973 Plymouth Roadrunner with a white stripe down the side. It looked just like the car from *Starsky & Hutch*, my favorite TV show, which I now was allowed to watch. I had a girlfriend, I was trying out for the football team at Southern Guilford High School in Greensboro and I was feeling the best I had felt since before my mother died.

Unlike the Pughs, the Steins didn't give a damn what I did. When I was a junior, I was dating the senior homecoming queen. The Steins did have a curfew and one night I was late after my date with the queen.

When I came home, I parked a block and a half away from the house and started pushing the muscle-car uphill to the house so the noise would not wake them up. I guided it to my regular parking spot along the curb and jumped the back yard fence. I lived in a tiny studio apartment that was without a bathroom or kitchen in the back of the house, so I didn't have to go inside. I was tiptoeing through the grass to get to my door when a loud voice suddenly boomed out from the darkness.

"Son, what the hell's wrong with you? You're in the goddamn grass so you don't have to tiptoe, dumbass."

That was Bill. He was a laid-back country guy. He didn't get mad; he just made fun of me.

The Steins were important in my life because they allowed me to develop socially. On the Pugh farm, other than church and tobacco fields, that didn't happen. I know I wouldn't have laughed as much, had girlfriends or have been able to develop some of my athletic skills had I not been allowed to move in with the Steins.

* * *

When I was 10 years old, I was on a playground where a baseball team was practicing and I decided to try out. But the first time someone threw the ball, I had my glove too low. The ball went over it and hit me flush in the face. I quit immediately.

Later, I started playing softball and I was pretty good. I didn't realize those skills transferred to baseball, but the first time I played baseball again, I was 16 and could throw the hell out of the ball, maybe because of throwing so many rocks at street signs while living with the Pughs. I said to myself, "Damn, I wish someone would have showed me how to do this stuff when I was 10." That's where not having a father then and later really affected my life.

Because of my mom's obsession with Dean Smith and North Carolina, I was a pretty good basketball player, although I didn't realize how good I was. I never had the chance to find out because on the first day of junior high school tryouts – when the gym was full of guys wanting to make the team – our first drill was layups and I jumped off the wrong foot. I guess I looked uncoordinated and they were trying to quickly weed out kids who could not play, so I was immediately and brutally cut. That doesn't do much for the ego. They didn't even let me take one shot.

But I had the last word. In my last year in high school, the seniors played the faculty in a basketball game for charity. I played with a vengeance and scored 27 points. The basketball coach came up to me after the game and asked, "Where in the hell have you been all my life? We could have used you." And my thought was: "I could have used a dad."

After I got cut, I settled on football and wrestling and had my share of successes. I don't remember Bill Stein trying to motivate me or encourage me to excel, but he did give me freedom. He did not become a mentor because he simply was not the type. But he was easy-going, lenient, generous and comically funny. And he loved his beer. When he had a few too many, which was often, he would get upset at the silliest things. Like the TV. If something came on that he did not like, he'd take out his pistol and shoot it through the roof. The first time he did it, it scared the hell out of me. But his wife Shelby said, "Don't worry about it. He's just drunk. But all you kids get out of the house for a while."

I'm sure if I had stayed at the Pughs, I would have had little opportunity with girls. But Bill knew it was a natural thing in high school and he was all for it. It was, however, dangerous to bring a girl home to meet him.

Like all 16-year-olds I had a few pimples. So one day, I was at the house with friends, including several girls. Bill walked in the room and decided it was time to mess with me, so he said: "What are those goddamn bumps on your face?" I was horrified and couldn't think of anything to say. Neither could my friends. So Bill, with his own wicked sense of humor said: "If one of these girls here will give you some pussy, that acne will go away."

I'm guessing the girls had never heard that from a parent before.

Although I would later have an incident with the Steins that would cause problems, in high school they were good for me. And I was comfortable enough around them that when I was in the Marines and had time off, I would go back to their house and stay with them.

But while the Steins were far different from the Pughs, neither served a parental role. I have a friend who was an amazing attorney but when he was 50, he gave up law and started playing the guitar. I asked him why and he said the only reason he had become a lawyer was because his mom and dad wanted him to be one. I had no parent who had dreams for me. The Steins provided a place to sleep, food to eat and freedom to develop as a high school kid. But they did not help me with goals, dreams or aspirations.

Throughout school, my academic career was nonexistent because no one gave a damn. I was never once asked for a report card, never urged to take a course, never asked what I wanted to be in life. At the time I was blah about it because when you are a foster kid, you don't dream about the future or look at your circumstances and feel sorry for yourself. You think about whether or not you are going to get the next meal or have a bed to sleep in or have a school to go to because there were times when those things were in doubt. You don't think about the fact that you have no parental or sibling love because that died along with your mother, your brother's abuse and separation from your sister.

Top left: Mom in Italy, aged 18. Top right: Mom and her first husband, Clayton, in Mom's hometown of Bari, Italy. Bottom: My favorite picture of my beautiful mother as she was about to leave for America.

Mom posing like Betty Gable in upstate NY after arriving in America.

Above: Mom at Clayton's parents' house in NY.
Below: Mother and her sister Polly. Wasn't until I was 50 that I discovered my Aunt Polly made her way to Los Angeles and worked as an actress until her death in the late 80s, about the time I arrived in LA.

My dad, Rudy David Smith, looking a lot like Robert Kennedy.

Top: One of only five pictures of my Dad. Bottom: My one and only Christmas with both Mother and Father. Dad would be dead within months.

Top left: Sporting the fro to my prom in 1978. Top right: Me at eighteen with my favorite Foster Mom, Shelby, from the Stein family. Bottom: On the last day I was awarded my Dress Blues uniform from my Senior Drill Instructor, SSG Baker, as the top graduate from my 3rd Battalion training back at the beginning of my Marine career. Everything I do in life has been informed by this man, who was like a father to me. Semper Fi.

Winning a bodybuilding championship in 1986.

Top: Me in the blue trunks on the right, winning the title.

Bottom left: Training Mary Lou Retton at Gold's Gym in Myrtle Beach, SC 1986. Check out the horrible shoes and jeans and the T-shit that would become an omen.

Snapping a pic of Mickey on one of our rides down the Sunset Strip, early 90s.

When I was working, I was riding, when I wasn't, I was walking.

CHAPTER 3 - ATTACK OF THE PHONE BOOTHS

Kyle McKinley had graduated from Southern Guilford High a year before me. One day during my senior year, he visited school and it changed my life. He was dressed in a dazzling Army outfit and he had put on 30 pounds. His muscles were ripped and the uniform was starched and stunning. I was instantly in awe.

At the time, if you graduated from our high school, you probably weren't going to go to college so you had two choices - work for UPS or join the military. Kyle looked so distinguished that I not only had great respect for him, but also sought his advice. I asked him if he thought the service would be good for me, and knowing my background as a football player and wrestler, he said: "You definitely should enlist in the Marines. They have the coolest uniforms"

That did it. Kyle had total credibility with me, but that is another indication of how much direction I received from foster parents. My mentor was not an adult; it was a guy one year older than me who looked impressive in a uniform. I decided to enlist and while it was the best decision I had made in my life to that point, some of my pent up anger over losing my mother and the constant insecurity of my living conditions began to surface. It took four months, but when I acted out, I was as subtle as a grenade.

My first Marine experience produced a surprise. I took a physical and they discovered I had a sports hernia. The enlistment officer said they were still going to accept me, and that when I got to basic training, they were going have a Navy surgeon repair it.

They sent me to the base at Parris Island, South Carolina, for my initial training and I embraced the Marine life. I loved the physical activities and wasn't really bothered by the intimidation, threats and screaming of the drill sergeants. Matter of fact, I loved all of it. I was finally being held accountable by an adult father-like figure – a shrill and strict one. I found nothing in the Marines was as bad as being forced to live in multiple foster homes when you're nine years old. I welcomed the routine and discipline and I excelled there.

After a week, they told me they had scheduled the surgery, which would be followed by at least eight weeks spent in convalescence platoon. Although I had been there a very short period, I had gotten to know the other guys in Platoon 3064. My life had been so unsettled since my mom had died that when it was in my power, which it had seldom been, I resisted change. At that point, the military had offered me certainty. For the next six years, even though I was not yet sure where my permanent duty station would be, I knew I would be a Marine. That would mean a guaranteed place to sleep, plenty of food to eat, clothes to wear and the sort of permanence I did not have growing up. Even when I was with the Steins, there was always the possibility they would tire of having a foster kid and I would have to go somewhere else. But life as a Marine would be stable and I did not want change after one week. So I declined the surgery to stay with the guys I had already met.

That probably was a mistake since I did not get the hernia fixed for another 20 years. Yeah, I have high pain tolerance, which doesn't always translate into smart decisions. But I was able to make my own choice and that was the first time I was able to do that.

When I moved in with the Steins and they allowed me to drive, play football, date girls and eat decent meals, I did well. In my youth, there had been a lot of uncertainty and disappointment. It turned out, however, that I learned a lot from my experiences. I had developed a survivor instinct and in the Marines, that serves you well.

When recruits start basic training, they are battered verbally by drill sergeants and officers. It's by design, of course. The military wants soldiers to feel pressure every day because if there is a war, the pressure is going to be much worse. For me, however, basic training was fun because it was not even close to being combat. So the harassment didn't really bother me, although no one really likes to be yelled at all the time. To limit that as much as I could, I looked for ways to stay one step in front of the drill sergeants.

In the barracks, there were 20 bunks on each side and the drill sergeant's room was at the end of the building. Each morning, he would come out of his room with a big aluminum trashcan. He would look at his watch and as soon as it hit 4:30, he would throw the trash can down the squad bay and it sounded like thunder in your ear. The idea was to mimic battle conditions, like you were under attack while in a deep sleep.

It was an awful way to wake up, but that was only the start. You had exactly three minutes to get out of bed, get dressed, get your boots on, and toe the line next to your bunk. While you were putting on your uniform and making the bed, the guy, who was a 6-foot-6 Puerto Rican, would walk down the middle of the bay and with a heavy accent would say: “I’ve got a hard on for every one of you.” It was a scene straight out of a movie and he was the perfect character for the badass role.

He did it every morning but despite that, some guys never learned how to not be shocked when it happened. It took me about two nights. I figured that he’d come out at the same time each morning, so I trained myself to wake up at 4:15. That was nothing new for me. I learned how to get up and move working in the tobacco fields.

While everyone else continued to sleep, I would put on everything except my boots and climb back in bed. If you were late, you’d have to go to push-ups, sit-ups or run. I never did. So not only did that help teach me how to prepare for a challenge, it also gave the drill sergeant a good impression of me. And I had to do it without him realizing it because if I had been caught, it would have been like I was cheating and payback would be ugly.

Marine basic training is difficult for some, but I flourished in a way that I never had in my life. I finished No. 1 in my class and there were all sorts of perks. When the Third Battalion graduated in November 1978, I was the only one allowed to wear the Marine dress blue uniform at the ceremony. Everyone else was in green. I had a white hat, white gloves and blue trousers with the famous blood red stripe down the side. I got to meet the base commandant and lead the parade. Being the "Honor Graduate," I was also allowed to pick any job the Marine Corps had to offer.

Looking back, it was another time I wish I had a father to help guide me - a dad who had known me my entire life, knew what kind of person I was and would point me in the right direction. He would have known how much I loved my country and how pursuing a career in the CIA or some other intelligence agency would be the perfect goal for me. He would have seen me excel in my first stint as an 18-year-old Marine. I was in a unit with a 22-year-old ex-Penn State football player, many excellent black athletes from inner cities and the Deep South, robust farm boys and former soldiers from other military branches who were stepping up their game to become Marines. But I was better than all of them. I aced everything - studies, physical training and because of my teenage experience with the .22, I was a sharpshooter in rifle training. No one was better with an M-16 than me. If I had just had a dad, I could have taken much better advantage of what I had accomplished.

As the top Marine in my class, I was able to pick Military Occupational Specialty (MOS). There were no wars back then and one of the things I had thought about doing in the future was police work. So I chose to go to Military Police school, which was held in a hellhole of a place named Annistan, Alabama. And that's where the wheels began coming off, but not right away.

* * *

Motivated by my success at Parris Island, I attacked the challenges of military police training fiercely and confidently. Again, I finished as the top recruit in my class and you would figure with such a start, I would be on my way to a distinguished stint as an upstanding and proud Marine. Instead, I became a shitbird.

Shitbird (noun): A completely useless individual who is unaware of his/her own complete uselessness.
(Source: Urban Dictionary)

"Shitbird is a synonym for dickhead, loser, slacker and deadbeat."
(Source: Military online chat room)

Fortunately, my tenure as a shitbird was very brief. Looking back, there was no doubt that at the time, I was in a period of experimenting. Considering what I had already been through in life, maybe Marine training was too easy. I got bored.

My permanent duty station was the Marine Corps Air Station at Cherry Point, North Carolina. I was an MP but instead of building on the success I'd had, I became cocky. I had proven I was great, or so I thought, but since I had served only six months of a six-year commitment, celebrating my brilliance was a little premature. It's like scoring six runs in the first inning of a baseball game. You don't stop playing.

My first bout with trouble came after I met a guy named Johnny, who was from Philadelphia. Despite my achievements, I was still a follower at that point. Again, I had never had anyone to teach me the concept of leadership, or to urge me to be a leader, so it's something I had to learn on my own. I'm just lucky that the lessons didn't include a long period of time in the brig or worse.

Johnny had seen a flashy Camaro driving around the base and when he told me he thought it would be a good idea to steal the tires, it sounded exciting so I was all in. He and another guy did the honors while I served as a lookout. It was one thing to steal them, but then quite another - and very ignorant - to put them on Johnny's car and drive around the base. The Camaro owner had reported the theft and my fellow MPs were watching out for the wheels, so he was easy to catch.

Johnny paid a big price. He was court-martialed, had to spend 30 days in the brig and got a dishonorable discharge. I was also brought up on charges because I helped him. But when one of the officers asked Johnny about me, Johnny said we were friends but I had not been with him that night. He didn't drop a dime on me and since he was the only witness, they had to let me go. I never saw him again after that. I guess he served 30 days in the brig and then went back to Pennsylvania. It's funny. At the time, I thought I had learned something not only about not ratting on your friends, but also about taking responsibility for your actions. But in thinking back, I guess I already knew it because when I was nine years old and the cop wanted me to rat out my abusive brother, I did not. But this was an adult lesson, so I would later benefit from it.

* * *

You'd think I'd also benefit from the close call with the court martial, but I was 19 years old and the thrill of getting away with something so large made me feel bullet proof.

That led to a second court martial.

A year after the Camaro incident, our unit was sent on a training exercise to the Marine Corps Air Ground Combat Center in a town named Twentynine Palms, California. We were supposed to undergo war training, even though we were not at war at the time. The military is always in a state of preparedness so even though we did not take it too seriously, we had no choice except to go through the training.

It was a boring assignment, which led one day to me acting like the ultimate shitbird and having what I thought was a brilliant idea. I decided that an afternoon of fun would be to take a jeep, drive into town, go to a Mexican fast food joint and buy some quesadillas and a case of beer. On the way back, I decided to entertain myself by shooting phone booths with an M-16. I had convinced a friend to assist me and his reward after we were caught and charged was a flight with me on a C-130 back to North Carolina for a court martial.

It looked for sure like I would get a dishonorable discharge, but fortunately, whoever was in charge of the evidence screwed it up royally. The casings from the rounds I fired at the phone booths – the only evidence in the case – were not tagged properly so when they were transferred to North Carolina, they were either lost or no one knew what they were. We kept waiting for something to happen, but the case just dried up. So the charges were dropped and I was back with my unit again, one lucky Marine

In looking back now, both incidents scare the hell out of me. When you get a dishonorable discharge, you lose a lot of civil rights. You can't vote, you can't own guns. It's the equivalent of a felony in some ways. It would have been sad for youthful ignorance to result in a loss of rights, but, thank God, I finally got a break in my life.

At the time, not surprisingly, they decided I was not MP material anymore and my penance was an assignment as the base dog catcher. There certainly could have been worse assignments, but to their credit, they looked at the big picture. I had been the top recruit in my first two training assignments. I had made two poor decisions, but overall, I think they saw a Marine who had been successful, worked hard and had only a brief period of immaturity and shitbirdedness. In short, I think they thought I was a soldier worth salvaging.

I would imagine they also figured there was no way I could screw up the job of being a dog catcher. And if I didn't start behaving, from their point of view, there was always the chance I'd get bit by a rabid dog, get rabies and die.

For me, it was a fun job because I love animals. The first

assignment I gave myself was to train a German Sheppard I named Killer, owing to his very special skill set. Instead of catching other dogs – and there always seemed to be strays on the base, which is why they needed a dog catcher – he'd just attack and maul them, or worse. Killer rode everywhere in the front seat with me.

It's difficult looking back at that period of my life now and knowing that back then I was OK with Killer attacking other dogs. But it gets back to having anger issues, and it's something that originally reared its head when I was still just a boy.

When the Pughs allowed me to shoot the .22 rifle, I learned how to handle it pretty quickly. I became good at using it and that was bad news for birds on the farm.

We had this cherry tree in our yard and the birds loved the cherries. I got so good at shooting that I could take the head off of a bird which landed on the tree from 50 yards away.

I guess the birds got wise to the risk. They stopped coming by the cherry tree. But I still felt a need to release this thing inside me, so I would stalk my way through the forest by the farm and would kill every bird I saw.

Way deep in the woods, I built this stone tomb for the dead birds. I think like one summer, I killed about 600 birds and put them all into it. I would also take some of their bones and make giant skeletons of monster birds.

It's nothing I'm proud of. I was in a very dark place. For some reason – extreme bitterness would be a good guess – I just enjoyed killing as many birds as I could. I think I was showing signs of becoming a serial killer because I've read that serial killers abuse animals and wet the bed and that was me back then.

I was obviously very, very fucked up at the time.

When I was 16 and still on the Pugh farm, I was walking through the snow and I saw deer footprints. So I decided to track the deer and finally spotted him about 75 yards ahead of me. It was cold – so cold that I could see his breath.

I got a little closer and then steadied myself to take the shot.

I took him down easy.

I dropped my rifle and ran to my kill. I placed my hands on the deer's chest and could feel him quivering beneath me. Only a few seconds passed but it seemed much longer because he was in such obvious pain. He stopped quivering and finally died, his blood seeping out and making the snow look like cherry snow cones.

Suddenly, I felt terrible. I wished I could take it back. It was nothing like shooting birds. They are small and die right away. But this was a big beautiful animal that had been healthy and he obviously struggled before he died. It got to me. I felt such grief.

After that, I never killed another thing, unless you count an M-16 taking out a phone booth. But nothing living or breathing.

* * *

I did find an outlet for some of my aggression on the football field. On each base they have a team and in our league, there were eight teams. There were some ex-college players on the team so it was good football, equivalent probably to a semi-pro team. I played defensive end and fullback. In high school, I had tried to play fullback, but the first time they handed me the ball, before I got hit, I closed my eyes and they saw it. So I was cut the first year. But then they moved me to guard on offense and linebacker on defense and I played two years and played well.

By the time I played Marine football, I had found the gym and bulked up from the 165 pounds I had weighed in high school to 230. I was determined to play fullback and I did earn a starting position. But since we didn't run the ball much, my carries were at a minimum.

Greenville, North Carolina, was about an hour away from Cherry Point and that was the home of East Carolina University. The head football coach was Ed Emory and he used to have yearly tryouts for walk-on players. It was open to players in the military and several of us decided to try out. The possibility intrigued me. I had never thought about going to college and no foster parent ever told me I should, so it was something I came up with on my own.

East Carolina was known as the Pirates and had beautiful purple and gold uniforms. The tryouts were a couple of months before I was going to be discharged. If I made it a walk-on, I could leave the Marines, enroll in school and play football. Unfortunately, I broke my ankle on the second drill and couldn't play anymore.

I had been confident that I could make the team. I was in the best shape of my life to that point. My 230 pounds was all muscle and that was because of the last job I had in the Marines.

My superiors at the base had no problem with my dog catcher performance but they decided I was not busy enough and they wanted to find something to keep me out of trouble. They obviously knew that I had a spotty record, but they also saw how much I had changed my body by working in the gym. So they decided to make me the noncommissioned training officer. My job was to be in charge of the battalion physical training, keep all the records, oversee the physical tests, keep everyone in shape and not let them get overweight.

I had quite the interesting record. As a military policeman, I had been almost court-martialed twice so I screwed that up. As the dog catcher, however, my performance was good so I think they made the decision to keep encouraging me to make good choices. They knew that I spent a lot of time in the gym and worked hard on my body. I had become this big buffed dude, looked sharp in uniform and had demonstrated that in the right situation, I performed as well as any Marine in my class.

My interest in body building actually began in high school when I read a story about Casey Viator, who at age 19 was the youngest man to ever win the Mr. America title. And then Kyle McKinley visited the high school and obviously had benefitted from weight work in the Army. I was already very active in the gym when they put me in charge of physical training, which allowed me to spend hours and hours working on my body. That's where body building became a life-long endeavor and provided me with a profession that would enable me to move to California, where I would discover yoga. And it was a fun profession. My job was to regularly kick ass and I found I could do that very well. And as an added bonus, a certain Major's estranged wife took a liking to me.

But that's all I'll say about that. Gentlemen never tell.

CHAPTER 4 - REDNECKS & ELTON JOHN

About a year before I got out of the Marines, I found my way to Atlantic Beach, North Carolina, which was about 20 miles from the base. The primary industry was tourism and although I was unaware of any requirement that only rednecks could vacation there, only rednecks vacationed there.

The perfect symbol of the town was the Country & Western bar that had the mandatory bucking bronco and a bunch of drunk cowboys proving their manhood by mastering the machine. Some of them were rodeo veterans and they were a rough bunch. When rodeo cowboys get drunk and want to fight, they are a challenge. They're like hockey players - not always the biggest guys but always the toughest. These guys ride wild bulls in their day job. Fighting a human in their leisure hours - even one bigger than them - is a favorite activity, second only to chasing cowgirls.

I was 21 and a year from getting out of the Marines and my job had regular hours during the day. So I took a part-time job as a bouncer and worked nights and weekends. One of the reasons I couldn't wait to get out of the Marines was so I could grow my hair and look normal. You had to have a jarhead haircut, and that was a problem off the base because you were kind of stigmatized. Guys didn't like you and it was not one of those periods where military guys were appealing to girls. When I was 19, 20, 21 years old, I wanted to hang out with the local kids, who were either military brats or just lived close by, and I did not want to be labeled only because of my hair.

So I started pushing the envelope and didn't shave the hair on the side of my head. I guess as long as I was working and behaving, my superiors lived with it. I was less self-conscious in social situations and began hanging out with a fun group. We spent a lot of time on the beach, playing volleyball, winning the tug of war championship and enjoying the summer weather. My girlfriend at the time was the local high school homecoming queen named Sofia, who went to Auburn where she became a cheerleader. We had one great summer together in1982 and when she left for school, Miss North Carolina USA moved into town and took Sofia's place. That made the fall of '82 pretty spectacular.

Women aside, that turned out to be an important period in my life. I learned the basics of bouncing, working at several bars because the jobs were not fulltime. I didn't realize it, but I was learning a profession that would not only allow me to make a living when I got out of the Marines, but also would enable me to move to California.

On that redneck beach in South Carolina, something dramatic happened. For the first time, I dreamed of the future and of becoming a success. In a *Playboy* magazine article, I read about Gavin de Becker, who was in the early stages of building what became the top security firm in Los Angeles. For the last 35 years, he has handled threat assessments for everyone from celebrities to politicians to the CIA. Although my performance as a military policeman had been less than stellar, I always thought a police career was a possibility for me. Ultimately, it became a backup plan. I wasn't sure what I wanted to be but if I couldn't do whatever it was, I could always be a cop.

When I read about Gavin de Becker, I was intrigued. I was already in the equivalent of an entry level position in the protection business. It was exciting to realize that it could not only be a job but also a very prestigious position. I didn't think of it as a goal on that day, but it became a permanent thought in the back of my mind. And later when I did move to California, I said to myself, "I'm going to join that Gavin guy's company and become a bodyguard for the superstars." In hindsight, it gave me a vocation when I left the military. So that bouncing job with the country clubs in the rock 'n roll bars proved to be a big deal.

* * *

Bouncing was good because I could multitask – let out a lot of anger and have a job at the same time. I had to bounce a lot of people and I really enjoyed it. I was always looking for a fight and in clubs like those, it's not hard to find one. If I was in the mood, I could turn a small offense into a felony. I could be standing next to a guy who was obnoxious and even if he wasn't doing anything wrong, I'd act like he was and say something like "What did you say to her? It's time for you to go." When he resisted, punches started flying. I could easily find a fight within seconds.

The bouncer job had a lot of perks. The girls liked tough guys and scoring with them was almost too easy. The bartenders were my friends and gave me and my girls free drinks. And as a bonus, I got to teach a few worthless pricks some manners, although I will admit I got my ass kicked a number of times. But I didn't care. I just enjoyed fighting. A funny thing about the South is that you get in a fight and many times, win or lose, you become friends with the guy you're fighting. It's an honor thing and you see it these days in the mixed martial arts fighting that has become so popular. I guess we were ahead of the times.

After I got out of the Marines, I decided to join the Greensboro Police Department. My record in the military didn't follow me because I got an honorable discharge. So people did not know about the two court martials. I was never convicted, anyway, so I did not need references. I just gave them my discharge and they said: "Military Policeman. That's great." The discharge didn't even say anything about dogcatcher or trainer. It was all MP.

I was stationed only four hours from home so a little before I was discharged, I drove to Greensboro, took the psychological test to become a policeman and passed. At the time, I was staying with the Steins. I lived them from ages 16 to 18 and they were so good to me that even when I went home for leave, I would go to their house. The Steins had a son and a daughter and they were closer to me than my own sister and brother. So I could go there any time I wanted and they let me stay there even though they weren't getting paid for it since I was out of the foster care system.

I passed the test to join the Greensboro Police Department and they said they would hire me but I had to take a physical first. I had never gotten the hernia fixed in the Marines, which wasn't very bright, so I was disqualified. And so I thought that had ended my police career.

The summer after I got out of the service I lived on the beach and bounced. But in October, the beach business dries up because it's a seasonal thing. I had a bankroll of about $300 so I went back to Greensboro and started waiting tables at a Mexican restaurant.

When my mother died the only thing I got was $4,000 and I received that from Social Security when I was 18. At the time, I found this 1968 Corvette that had a 427 big block engine and the guy just happened to be selling it for $4,000. So I bought it and drove it during my last year of high school and two years of the Marines. But I didn't take care of it. I trashed it so badly that I finally just left in the back yard of a buddy's house with the engine blown. One day, I got a phone call and a guy asked me if I owned a '68 Corvette. The smart thing, of course, would have been to keep the car. It was a convertible and it is worth a lot of money now, probably $50,000. But the guy offered me $3,000 and it would have cost more than that to repair it, so I didn't think twice. I sold it.

Oddly, that led to a split-up between the Steins and me. Bill and Shelby did not have a lot of money, which was one reason they took in foster children. I sold the Corvette when I was still in the Marines and at the time, my living expenses, food, clothes, etc., were covered. On one trip home, the Steins said they had found a bar that was available to buy but they couldn't open it because they did not have $1,500 for the liquor license. So, being flush with money, I loaned it to them. They said they would pay it back as quickly as they could, but never did. I was still spending my off-time there so I didn't want to make a big deal out of it because they could have told me not to stay there anymore.

But after I got out of the Marines, I became more and more resentful when they did not pay me back. So one night, a friend of mine named Sonny told me he was leaving that night to move to South Carolina and I said, "I'll go with you." I went home, put all my stuff in a duffel bag, put it in the back of his Volkswagen and at 5 a.m., we left for South Carolina without telling the Steins anything or saying goodbye. I didn't see them again for 30 years.

* * *

Sonny and I moved to Myrtle Beach but we had only a couple of hundred bucks between us. We had a friend to live with, but I had to sleep on the floor in his apartment. I had two job skills at the time – bouncing and working in a restaurant. I met a guy who had a job at a place named the Mayor's House, which advertised itself as a "fine dining establishment." In hindsight, it was a huge scam. The food was not bad, but it was nothing special and way overpriced. Myrtle Beach is a resort and a place designed to take advantage of wealthy tourists. There are more than 100 golf courses in the greater Myrtle Beach area and unlike Atlantic Beach where I first worked as a bouncer, there aren't a lot of rednecks who play golf.

The Mayor's House was dedicated to taking as much money as it possibly could from the rich people. Dinner for two could run more than $200. Dinner for six was closer to $1,000 and there were bottles of wine that probably sold for $20 in a store but were over $100 in the restaurant.

I did, however, have my first experience with a heroin addict, whose name was George. He was the most accomplished waiter in the place and he taught me how to wait tables like I was a captain. It was an invaluable experience. I ended up making as much as $400 in tips in a night and I was 23 years old. That was a job that carried me for two or three years. But then I started getting the itch again to be a cop so I went down to the Myrtle Beach Police Department to apply.

I had met a guy who eventually became chief of police and told him about my experience in the Marines, leaving out, of course, the stolen wheels and bullet-riddled phone booths. He set me up with an interview and I got the job, although I had to pass a physical and that was going to be a problem. Or so I thought.

I found out that a woman I had met happened to work for a doctor who did all of the police physicals. She made an appointment and when I got to his office, he just sat across from me, asked a few questions and then said, "Everything looks good to me." I think he was getting a nice paycheck to handle medical matters for the police department and simply did not care, which was fine with me.

I was 26 and they said I was going to a training academy for six months. I had already been to an academy in the military but they said that did not matter. If I wanted to work for them, I had to go to a civilian academy. I had no intention of spending six months working on something I already knew so instead, they assigned me to duty as a jailer, where I worked booking people, learning the procedure and meeting guys on the force.

Myrtle Beach was a typical tourist town and one of the ways it made money was by arresting people for public intoxication or open containers. Everybody would walk around the beach with a beer and a bunch of them would get arrested for having an open container. The jail needed a revolving door. They'd come in, I'd book them, they'd pay $40, I let them go back out and the transaction happened very quickly. I did that for six months and was going to continue doing that because the hours were regular and I had time for an off-duty job.

A new bar opened down the street from the jail and it was hiring bouncers so I could get part-time work to make more money. I applied for the job as head of security but they said there was a guy named Larry who was moving from Raleigh, North Carolina, and he had already been hired for the position. Larry had supposedly been a bodyguard for Elton John and, well, I had been a bodyguard for guys stealing wheels off a Camaro. So he had the edge in experience.

Larry showed up and it turned out that he was a cokehead. He got kicked out of the Marine Corps because of drugs, but that didn't faze him. He may have had a drug problem, but he was a natural born leader and everyone liked and respected him. I later met a lot of Hollywood stars, but Larry was the most charismatic guy I have ever met. People would follow him off a cliff, and I was one of those guys. I would do anything for Larry. He was a little bit older than me, and he was a big brother figure. He had his shit together, had a boat, had a Corvette and had a house on the water. I discovered Larry did not become wealthy working security, even if he had protected rock stars.

Larry was a major league drug dealer.

CHAPTER 5 - A GOOD TIME TO BE A BUFFOON

I found myself in a unique position with Larry. My day job was enforcing the law. At night, I spent my time with someone I knew was breaking the law. That's not exactly how they teach it at police academies.

But it was a reflection of Larry's magnetism. In describing special people, you often hear the term: *The It Factor*. Larry had "it" and he had it in spades. With my background, being around such a powerful personality was life-changing. It didn't take long for me to find out that when he wasn't working as the head of security for the nightclub, Larry was dealing drugs. That did not stop me from being around him and I never once considered dropping a dime on him.

He obviously saw that I was more loyal to him than I was to my career in law enforcement. That was evident one night when he asked me "You want to do some blow?"

I kind of laughed.

"Larry, you do know what my day job is, right?"

He shrugged.

"Do you feel like a cop right now? Like, at this very moment?"

"Not really," I said.

And I felt like less of one a few seconds later when I was standing in the stairwell of Streamers nightclub in Myrtle Beach, South Carolina, snorting the first line of many ounces of cocaine that I would inhale during the next three years.

Afterwards, he said casually that I should "quit that stupid job" and work fulltime security with him. I could make more money and not waste my time at the police academy. It seemed to make perfect sense, especially coming from a guy who had been so successful. So I said, "You're right, I'm tired of wearing uniforms anyway" and my career in law enforcement came to an abrupt and unspectacular end. It's strange what the rush of blow will do to your decision-making process.

While serving as Larry's unofficial bodyguard, I also picked up work as a bouncer at several clubs. During that time, he built a drug-running operation between Florida and South Carolina and I was riding shotgun with him in a haze of personal denial. I kept telling myself that I really wasn't the one dealing in pounds of coke; I was just watching my friend's back.

As you might imagine, we had many wild and crazy moments and it turned out my previous "stupid job" actually came in handy. About a week after I left the police department, Larry and I got into a fight with some guys at one of the clubs and Larry got hit on the head with a bottle. He recovered, but about a week later when we were working at another club, we were standing in the parking lot at 2 a.m.

Larry turned to me and said "Remember the guys we got into a fight with last week? Don't look now, but they're coming towards us."

I had been playing a game on a video machine and had just gotten a roll of quarters, which was good because the guy running towards me was about 6-foot-3 and weighed about 250. He was big, but not quick, so when he lunged at me, I sidestepped him, swung and hit him right in the face with the roll of quarters in my fist. He dropped like a bag of dirt. The other guy hit Larry in the back of the head with a beer bottle and glass was sticking out of Larry's hair. So the fight ended and I took Larry to the hospital.

When we got there, I realized in the excitement of the moment, I had forgotten that I was carrying a small bag of cocaine for Larry. But there was nothing I could do because the other guys happened to come to the same hospital. Larry saw them and told me they were in the next room, so I went crashing through the door and started beating the hell out of the guy as he was lying on the gurney. The hospital people quickly called the police and they got there pretty fast and arrested us.

Two weeks after leaving the police force, I end up in a cell in the jail where I had worked and I had a bag of cocaine on me. But all the guys who worked there were my friends, so they just laughed and let me out without patting me down.

If only they had known.

From 1986 to 1989, I hung out with Larry pretty much every night. When he became general manager of the club, I was promoted to the head of security. The whole time, he was dealing drugs.

He also kept a large stash for personal use, at least a kilo around the house, and we made regular use of it. I found out that I liked blow, but I never got hooked on it. I did it only because it was available and free – somewhat like the girls who followed us around.

Larry was like a kingpin and like all successful drug dealers, he always had an entourage. He would have parties at his huge house and he had a different way of decorating. For example, he kept a Harley-Davidson in the living room. I'm not sure why, but it was a hell of a conversation piece. For fun, I'd crank it up and ride it around the pool table. Like I said, it was a big house.

There were easily more than 100 people attending on any given night and the parties would go on until daybreak. It was a carefree life and all I had to do was watch Larry's back. There was not much of a long-term future in it, but for that three-year period it was a lot of fun.

* * *

One day, Larry delivered some stunning news. In one breath, he told me he had broken up with his girlfriend and in the next, he announced matter-of-factly that he was moving to California. The first thought that went through my mind was the article on Gavin de Becker that I had read when I was in the Marines. His company was in L.A. and for several years, I had wanted to go to California. When Larry told me he would give me $5,000 if I would move with him, the decision was made. We took off cross-country, found our way to Oxnard, 60 miles northwest of Los Angeles, rented a house on the beach and suddenly, we were eating lobster every night.

Three months later, however, we were out of money and Larry surprised me again, this time announcing he was getting back together with his girlfriend and he was going to return to South Carolina to resume his dealing. At that point, I did not want to leave California so I told Larry although he had put me in a lousy position, I was moving south to Los Angeles.

Larry was always thinking, always lining up a plan. He knew I'd be unhappy, but he was prepared. He said he would make it up to me and then told me he had arranged a drug deal in South Carolina between two guys who did not know each other. If I handled it for him, it would be worth $5,000 to me.

I wanted no part of it.

But...

I needed the money.

And you already know how I earned it.

* * *

Larry left California and I didn't see him for a long time because unknown to me, he got caught dealing drugs and went to prison for five years. I found out some of the details years later when he called me out of the blue and said he was in L.A.

I met him in a bar on Hollywood Boulevard one afternoon and Larry casually told me I had narrowly avoided big trouble myself.

"The DEA agents were looking for you," he said. "They had pictures of you and me at a drug deal and that's how they busted me. They asked about you and wanted to find this ex-cop turned bad. I told them you were just a buffoon who hung out with me sometimes. I said you had nothing to do with anything."

Although I wasn't real wild about the way he described me, I was thankful that he had not given me up. It was another time I narrowly escaped being busted with a friend who covered for me. He might have been able to save his own ass had he cooperated with the authorities. But he didn't and I'll never forget that.

There are a number of tales like this that Larry and I shared, successful drug deals, and deals gone bad. Guns pulled, teeth lost, lives ruined.

The last time I saw Larry was in L.A. in 1997 when I was working and spending a lot of time with Mickey Rourke, the actor, who was a friend of mine. Larry was in town and wanted to run a "deal" by me. Mickey, liking a good caper as much as the next guy, said we could talk at his house on Crescent Heights in West Hollywood.

When Larry arrived, I was shocked. He was snorting meth and his body was shaking and broken. But beneath it all, in my eyes anyway, he still had the magic. I was in whatever he wanted to do until he told us the plan. He wanted Mick and me to look at $50,000 in counterfeit $20 bills that Larry had made himself. We agreed the money looked real enough at first glance.

Larry's plan was to go to east L.A. and do a deal with a Mexican group he had found. I knew that was dangerous and told him it was a terrible idea. I stalled him by saying he should think about it and that I wanted to go to yoga.

"Yoga?" Larry asked with a snarl.

"Yeah, yoga," I said.

I told him after he slept on his idea that if he still felt like going the next day, I'd have his back. He said OK and left with a couple of signed 8x10 headshots of Mickey.

When I got back from yoga I had a message from Larry waiting for me on my answer phone.

"Hey man, my connection said it had to be done tonight. I'll call you when I get back. Dinner's on me tonight, buddy."

I never heard from or saw my friend again.

CHAPTER 6 - ABANDONED BY THE DRUG DEALER

I was 29 years old when I moved with Larry to California and I was spectacularly unskilled in the art of clear thinking. Having five grand in my pocket was comforting, but I knew it wouldn't last forever. I was an experienced bouncer and there were far more bars and night clubs in Los Angeles than in South Carolina. So that was an obvious starting point. Larry was also an accomplished drug dealer although that is not a very safe or stable profession. But it would pay the bills.

In the Marines, I had learned the importance of having a backup plan. So while driving to L.A. with a major drug trafficker, I developed Plan B, which was to apply to the Los Angeles Police Department.

That is correct. My serious contemplation of how I was going to earn money consisted of two options – break the law, or enforce it. And I don't remember thinking for one second that it was idiotic to have career choices that contradicted each other. It was yet another example of how sorely I missed having the influence of a father or father figure. My only minor role model was Bill Stein, a comic book character who drank too much beer, shot holes in the ceiling when he was angry and encouraged teenage girls to be generous with pussy. My maturity was at a high school level at best and as I like to tell my yoga students and say about myself now, I have always been 10 years behind on everything, a late bloomer in every sense.

When Larry bolted and I had nothing, I again considered applying at the LAPD. To this day I am pro-police. I've taught yoga to the Santa Monica SWAT team, whose members liked me so much that they called me "Alpha dog" after a class one day. I was flattered but also a little sad because it made me think of what might have been.

I have met and became friends with many officers and if ever needed, I'd have their back. I always thought that L.A. would be the coolest place in the country to be a policeman. L.A. cops were like superheroes. They were stars. Think about all the L.A. cop shows on TV or in the movies – *Dragnet, Colombo, Police Story, Die Hard, The Terminator.* The heroes were Hollywood's lawmen. What could be more glamorous and exciting?

Being a cop is a powerful position that attracts a different type of personality. You seldom see young men trying to decide if they'd rather be cops or doctors, cops or engineers, cops or bankers. There is no doubt that some cops have criminal tendencies, not because they shoot people or do dirty things, but because it just takes a different type of animal to do the job.

When fighting criminals, you have to think like them, so there's a fine line there. One of the reasons people are drawn to police work is that it is one of the few gigs in the world where you can legally carry a gun openly, which is primal macho stuff. You can park in the red zone, drive as fast as you want and fuck with people if you're bored – like I did in the Marines. That's a lot of power for a guy who typically has a high school education, criminal justice degree or is just out of the military. People seldom fuck with cops. It doesn't matter if you are a billionaire or a bartender. If you're driving and see a cop, you're nervous. If you're acting like an ass, you stop. That power is enticing for a lot of people who aren't qualified to do anything else. Don't get me wrong – there are many brilliant cops who are in law enforcement because they are dedicated civil servants. But there is a reason the saying "cops make the best criminals and criminals make the best cops."

* * *

When Larry left, however, being a cop was still Plan B because I had no money, no place to live and no desire to go back and ask the Steins for a place to stay. I had my restaurant experience so I found a high-end place called the Chart House and it had an opening. It was in Malibu, a great location, but the only job available was as the salad bar boy until you paid your dues to get the higher paying waiter jobs.

The salad boy? Really? Damn.

Pride aside, desperate times require desperate measures, so for three months, I spent my days and nights filling up the vegetable bins, the salad dressings, the croutons, the shredded cheese, etc. The best part of the job was that it was close to Pepperdine University and all the beautiful college girls worked part-time at the restaurant. But I was a former Marine, a badass bouncer, a cop and all-around mother fucker and I was filling the ranch dressing? It took a couple of months, but I finally lost what dignity I had left, so I left.

I happened to know one person in L.A. who I thought might be able to help me, a man named Stefanos Miltsakakis. We had been great friends when we met at Myrtle Beach. Stefanos was this big, hulking Greek guy who had qualified for the 1984 Greece Olympic wrestling team but did not participate because of a knee injury. He had a wrestling scholarship to North Carolina State and later trained in Brazilian Vale Tudo, which is similar to Mixed Martial Arts, and won a world championship.

He decided to try acting and got his first break in 1989 when he auditioned for a part in the Jean-Claude Van Damme movie *Cyborg* and got the role. That was his first film and the beginning of his career as a movie villain. Part of the movie was shot in South Carolina but after the crew left, Stephanos stayed and was a bouncer at the same club where I worked. I appreciated him right away.

One night, I got in a fight with a tough guy who was kicking my ass. He was huge, much bigger than me, and he pinned me to the ground. He was banging away at me and all I could see was the black of night, which turned out to be his t-shirt. Next thing I know, I saw stars in the sky because Stephanos came to my rescue. He just picked this guy up, which dislocated his shoulder, and tossed him aside. He was probably the toughest, baddest man I've ever seen in my life, even to this day, although he's probably lost a muscle or two as he's aged.

After Larry left, I managed to get Stefanos' phone number, called him and told him I needed help. He said he'd heard I was in L.A. – I have no idea how – and I could stay with him. He had a place on Wilshire Boulevard and he let me crash there for three days. He also got me a job at a bar making $100 a night as a bouncer.

So the cop plan was put on hold and I was back in the world of bouncing. And that actually was the beginning of my direct journey to yoga. Larry was gone and I was going to find that bouncing in high class Los Angeles clubs is far more prestigious that in redneck bars or scam high-end places in South Carolina.

But that was later. At first, Stefanos got me jobs at dive bars, including one that attracted people like Axl Rose, the lead singer for Guns 'N Roses. Rose would come in, get rowdy and Stefanos would snatch him up and throw him out the back door. It was before Rose and his group took off and became a big-name band.

Although $100 a night came in handy, it wasn't much when you work twice a week at two different clubs. But the specter of Larry and drugs had been removed and I loved L.A. right away. I did a good job at the first bar and I found that you can quickly build a reputation by word of mouth in L.A. I had grown up a little and didn't feel the need to fight as much as I had in South Carolina, although anywhere there is alcohol, young men and pretty women, there are going to be situations that can only be handled physically. But for the most part, I kept the peace and suddenly opportunities opened up at better bars. And the bouncer job actually opened the door to my brief and undistinguished career as an actor.

Pictures from my biker days.

Top: My chosen brothers. From left to right - Dimitris, myself, Craig Kilborn and Dr Chris Gronet.

Bottom: My Meisner drama class graduate pic from 1997. Me dead center, of course.

My modeling days working on a Ralph Lauren ad.

Publicity picture from my acting days.

Top: With Stanton Dodson, who let me live in his house high in the Hollywood Hills.
Bottom: My biggest yoga influence and the man who gave me my start, yoga rebel, Bryan Kest.

Top: From left to right, Freddy, Caresse, and Freddy's dad, Clayton, giving away my sister at her wedding.

Bottom: Bringing redneck chic to LA.

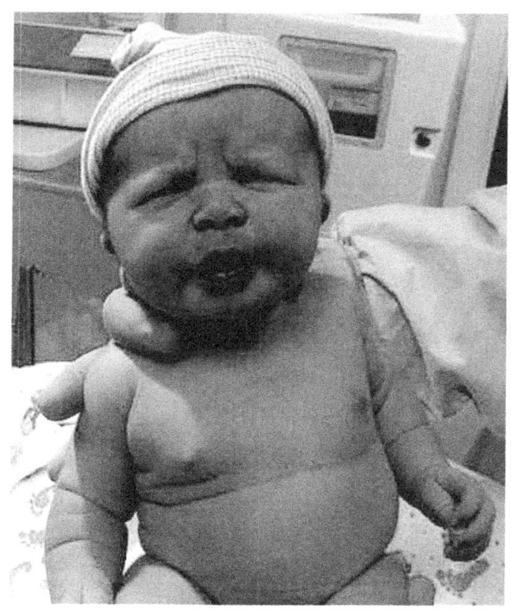

The day I found purpose - Scarlett 30 seconds into her own journey.

Scarlett Rose Smith.

The day before ending up in ICU with a heart scare.
Didn't see that coming.

Yoga.

CHAPTER 7 - MY JAMES BOND EXPERIENCE

Stefanos' acting career began to flourish and that was good news for me. At 6-foot-1 and 220 pounds of pure muscle, he was a menacing figure and became a popular bad guy in action movies. He was in five films with Jean Claude van Damme and one with Jet Li. After debuting in *Cyborg*, he got two more roles in 1989 and he gave up his night jobs to concentrate on fulltime acting.

So I took his place. I was gaining some notoriety at the time because as a bouncer, I was very good at preserving the peace, even if I had to kick a few asses to do it. With Stefanos gone, I was able to get a job at superhot club called Bar One on Sunset Blvd., located on the outskirts of West Hollywood near Beverly Hills. That's where I met and got to know many celebrities for the first time – Mark Wahlberg, Don Henley and Prince, who, I'm proud to report, once stole a girlfriend of mine.

Trendy bars often have a short shelf life in L.A. When a new club opens, it caters to the beautiful people and stars and it gets crazy. When a club is hot, the lines to get in are long. People will wait for hours for a chance to mingle with the stars.

At first, the new hip clubs attract the elite crowd – heavyweight actors, musicians, producers, directors and gangsters of every stripe. I was once questioned by the FBI about one of our guests, a man in the music industry who had pretty open mob connections and was so proud of what he did that he named his softball team "The Thugs" and invited me to play on it. I'll go ahead and keep his name a secret, however. I think you can understand why.

After a year or so in the limelight, hot bars cool down, a new place opens close by and the beautiful people get bored so they bolt. I saw it happen constantly and it's kind of humorous. With the A-list gone, the first bar is forced to welcome the B-list. Then it's the C-list because yet another bar opens. At that point, the first bar is doomed. The venue gets rougher, there are more arguments, more fights and it's no longer the place to be. I learned quickly not to stay anywhere too long and that enabled me to develop many contacts and to keep the cash flowing in.

As I kept moving up in the bar world, my reputation continued to grow because I became more sophisticated not only at solving problems, but also avoiding them. Clubs obviously want the image of being safe and although you can intimidate and handle troublemakers by making it known that you will kick their ass, avoiding problems is far more desirable.

When the House of Blues opened in West Hollywood, I was hired as head of security, had a staff of 25 working for me and I was very proactive in trying to identify and take care of problems before they had a chance to develop. One of the things I did was find a place upstairs where I could watch as people came in. I would profile mostly guys, not to discriminate, but rather as a way to spot someone who might have an excessive testosterone level.

If I saw someone who was dressed in such a way to bring attention to himself, or someone strutting around like he owned the place, I'd go downstairs and introduce myself and say, "Hey, my name is Rudy and I'm head of security. What's your name?" The guy would be suspicious, but then I'd say, "Listen my man, we get crowded here, but you look like a good guy and if there's ever any problem, just let me know. If anyone gives you a hard time, I'll take care of him."

You wouldn't believe how many times it worked. The guy I had talked to would have a problem, like someone pinching his girlfriend's ass, but instead of starting a fight, he'd come find me. I had given him ownership of the place and rather than get into a situation where he got kicked out - and maybe beat up - he would let me take care of it.

Guys would also keep their friends in line. If one of their pals started acting out and I had to confront him, the guy I had empowered would say, "Hey, let's be cool. This is Rudy and he's a good guy. He's head of security, so we're going to do whatever he says."

Although that's part of the skill of being a great bouncer, it also is reflective of yoga. Even though I had not learned a lot about yoga at the time, as I got older, I had learned the value of restraint. No matter how much you like to fight, it gets old and it hurts. So if you can figure a way to control the situation without sacrificing your manhood - or being a wimp - the result is much more pleasant and healthy. Restraint is a fundamental tenet of yoga.

My work as a bouncer and head of security led to another advancement for me. I became a doorman and club promoter and that is a powerful position in L.A. I once read in *Vanity Fair* that a nightclub doorman was the 25th most powerful person in Hollywood. I got a big kick out of that and my friends pricked me about it constantly.

I'm not sure of the exact ranking, but I do know the doorman has significant clout in the world of elite bars and restaurants. Although it may be surprising to some, there is a real science in deciding who gets in a club, who bypasses the line and I learned it quickly. Owners want the beautiful people in their clubs. They also want about a 55-45 ratio of women to men and I had a clicker so I could keep an accurate count. Any doorman who lets the club become a dick farm wouldn't have his job long. Being a doorman is how I met Sylvester Stallone, Henley, Wahlberg, Rourke, Sean Penn and, my biggest thrill, Marlon Brando. I'm proud to say I became the top doorman in L.A., and it was the way I handled that job that allowed me to get into acting so easily. I got to know many of the agents, producers, directors and casting people and that opened up a few opportunities for me.

The first big-time producers I met were Jerry Bruckheimer and the late Don Simpson. Jerry gave me my first acting job and my screen actors guild card. I got to know Michael Bay, who later directed me in my first film, *The Rock* with Sean Connery and Nicolas Cage. Bay later produced or directed *Armageddon, Pearl Harbor, The Texas Chainsaw Massacre, Transformers, Teenage Mutant Ninja Turtles, 13 Hours: The Secret Soldiers of Benghazi* and many more blockbusters. His ground-breaking work changed films forever, for better or worse, depending on your taste.

But at the time, he was just getting started, doing videos with singers like Tina Turner, Meat Loaf, Donnie Osmond and others. I knew who he was so one night, I pulled him out of line and said, "Come on in." He was five years younger than me, 26 years old at the time, and had just finished his masters at the Art Center College of Design in Pasadena. He was clearly on his way up. We became friends for many years until I became such a pain in the ass, trying to get jobs in his films during my desperate years as a would-be actor. He began avoiding me and, frankly, I don't blame him.

While working as a doorman, I developed a Rolodex of hundreds of phone numbers. When I went to a new club, I'd make strategic phone calls and celebrities would often come to the new place because they knew I would get them in immediately. I developed a reputation so when someone opened a new club, I would get hired because the owner wanted the rich and famous to come to his club.

The bouncer jobs were good for me because I was successful and it built my confidence and ego. The job also allowed me to multitask. If someone got out of line and wanted to fight, that would allow me to vent some anger – and I was getting paid.

But being a doorman and wearing expensive suits to work was much better because it cut way down on the fighting. As much as I liked to fight, sometimes it hurt like hell. For example, one night this dude took exception to me not allowing him into the club. He challenged me to a fight and, of course, I accepted. I handed my guest list to my assistant, stepped over the velvet rope between us and was ready to make quick work of this clown. Instead, he unleashed this roundhouse kick with his leg, caught me flush upside the head and knocked me out. When I woke up, I was in the middle of traffic on Sunset Blvd. I later found out that the guy was an Israeli commando on vacation in L.A.

Other than that mild setback, the doorman job was much less taxing on my body. I came to work looking very respectable, developed a reputation as an influential doorman, and I even made a gossip column in 1995 when *USA Today* named me the best bouncer/doorman in the U.S. I'm sure the source of that information was someone I had let in a club, but it was kind of funny and cool at the same time and it certainly didn't hurt my name recognition. And considering my past, feeling good about myself was a huge deal. Plus I had succeeded in California. I had nothing when I arrived there, but within a few years, I was making good money and mingling with people I used to watch in a Carolina movie theater.

The doorman jobs were very lucrative. I was making up to $1,000 a night, but more importantly making contacts and making high-level friends. Being around so many actors aroused my competitive instincts. I've always been extremely competitive and I still am. Use to be, if I saw yoga teachers who were getting some notoriety, it irritated the hell out me because I knew I was better than them. After meeting many actors – everyone from stars to B-level guys who thought they were talented but were not going anywhere – I decided to go to drama school. In my wildest dreams, I was going to become the next Brando – or at least a B-level guy who could make good bucks fucking around on film sets and having "lunch" with the cute extras in my honey wagon.

* * *

In 1995, Bay and Bruckheimer were about to film a new military-type movie and Bay, knowing that I was a Marine, asked me if I could play one.

"Of course," I said, thinking this was the break that I always knew was coming.

At the time, I was taking acting classes in Santa Monica at the Joanne Baron/D.W. Brown Studio. The program was based on the Sanford Meisner acting theory and it was a very prestigious school. I was serious about my craft, so I figured the two-year program was the best way to improve my acting skills.

It was a demanding school. I was working as a doorman at nights and then going to school for five hours during the day. But I thought it was paying off when I got to audition for *The Rock* and read for the part of a Marine. I thought I had a sure thing when Bruckheimer told the casting director, "Now, that's what a Marine looks like." I was surprised and disappointed, however, when I didn't get that role. But my feeling that I had done well proved to be correct. They offered me another part as a helicopter pilot and we shot the scenes for that. A few months after the shoot, however,

Michael Bay called to say, "I've got some bad news for you, Rudy. Your part ended up on the cutting room floor. Sorry."

Despite that, I was encouraged. Sean Connery was a hero of mine from his days as James Bond. On one of the days my scenes were being filmed, I was sitting in a trailer getting makeup and the door flings open. I look in the mirror and in glides Sean Connery. He has a white robe on but it was not covering the top of his big, furry chest. He sat down right next to me and said in his famous Scottish accent, "If I was as handsome as this young man, I wouldn't need any makeup at all." I was blown away. But they got me out of there quick so they could do his hair and makeup.

I was also there for a hilarious behind-the-scenes moment with Connery and Nick Cage. They were talking to Michael Bay and Cage had a wetsuit on because in the scene, he was going to jump in the water and swim to Alcatraz. A large air tank was attached to his chest and the whole look was very bulky. Meanwhile, Connery is there in a sleek, expensive wetsuit, his beard trimmed perfectly and he looks magnificent - cultured and stylish like he was still playing 007. Nick was staring at him, looking him up and down and was clearly irritated. It's bad enough being on screen with a guy who had been a sex symbol for 30 years, but the frumpy, baggy wetsuit made it worse.

When Nick gets excited, he talks real fast and so he started spitting out words at Bay.

"Let me ask you this, Mike," he said. "I look at Mr. Connery and he looks like James Bond. I look like a fucking idiot. Why is that?"

Michael explained that when Nick went in the water because of the water pressure he was going to need the air tank. So Cage said, "Fine. But for the one percent of the audience that will understand this, do I have to wear this tank and look like a fool?"

So Sean Connery smiled and said "Well, that's not the worst part. You are actually going to dive into the water and when I start to go towards the water we are going to cut and then we'll pick it up where you come out of the water and I'm already out and helping pull you up and out of the water."

Cage was totally exasperated, too wound up to see Connery was having a good time messing with him. It was pretty funny to watch up close from two feet away.

* * *

As Michael continued to gain stature and produce and direct great movies, he also continued coming to clubs where I worked. I would obviously usher him in right away although by then, everyone knew who he was.

He also told me once that he needed an assistant. I had a roommate named Kimberly and told him she'd be great. Off my recommendation, she got the job. One day, she told me: "Rudy, I was in Michael's office and he has a list of actors. And your name is on the list." At the time it was an achievement that made me very proud and gave me some hope. I had come a long way from the pig farm.

Unfortunately, that was in the days before cell phones became common and I had a pager. But I didn't pay close enough attention to it and found out later that I had missed being able to audition for two of Michael's movies because they couldn't get in touch with me. At my level, the most important thing was to be available. Michael is very impatient, so Kimberly said he'd be in his office and yell out, "Get me (whoever) and get him here right now." When I didn't respond, they simply went to the next name on the list.

My best role – again, a brief one – was a speaking part in *Armageddon,* which had a sensational cast: Bruce Willis, my friend Billy Bob Thornton, Ben Affleck, Liv Tyler, Steve Buscemi, William Fichtner and Owen Wilson. I played an FBI agent and my speaking part was with Will Patton, who has been in many great movies including *Remember the Titans, Entrapment* and *The Client.*

I did find out that Bay's reputation as running a tight set was well founded. Before one of the scenes, the actors were late getting to the set and Michael was pissed off and yelling to an assistant, "Where are the fucking actors! Get them in here!" So I smiled and said, "Michael I'm right behind you." He turned, gave me a faint smile – but only for a second – and said, "Oh, hey Rudy. Thanks for being on time."

* * *

I also became close friends with Mickey Rourke and he became for me a little like Larry, the drug dealer – not because of drugs, but because of his charisma. I had admired Mickey from afar for many years before I met him and it was certainly fun to be around him. It was amazing to become friends with him and watch him break down a script and his role in it. For an actor like me, it was a master's class like none other because to this day I think he may be one of the top five actors in movie history. More importantly, I also quickly learned that Mickey is the type of man who would give you the shirt off his back and his last dollar bill. He is truly one of my all-time favorites.

I served as an unofficial bodyguard for him, which included driving duties. One day, I was taking him to a set where he was going to start shooting a movie that had Dennis Hopper as the lead actor. There was no role for me in the movie, but Mickey got me a job as his assistant.

We got to the set and Mickey sat in a chair petting one of his Chihuahua dogs that he took everywhere with him. The dog was named Chocolate and Mickey got so attached to him that I thought he might kill himself later when the dog died. As they prepared to start filming, the door opened and someone walked in but Mickey couldn't see who it was because the sun was behind the guy. It turned out to be Hopper, but not knowing that and blinded by the sun in his eyes, Mickey shouted, "Who in the hell is that?" Apparently, that really irritated the director, although we didn't know why, but he snapped at Mickey, "It's Dennis Hopper."

About an hour later, he called Mickey into his office. He

thought Mickey was drunk and Mickey may have been since he was on a self-destructive path at the time. This was years before Mickey made his comeback with the role in *The Wrestler* and got an Academy Award nomination for Best Actor. At the time he was not getting many great roles, hardly working at all. He was about 45 and had nothing emotionally, spiritually, financially or physically. He was really down and he thought he was finished. So the last thing he needed was an angry director, and as it turns out, that was the last thing I needed, too.

The director at least made it quick. He reamed Mickey for a few seconds and then said, "You're fired . . . and take Rudy with you!"

I wanted to say, "What the hell did I do?" But it didn't matter. I was guilty by association. The connection that helped me get the job also led to me losing it.

* * *

I continued working as a doorman and I was also chasing auditions. I had speaking roles in eight films and I also got work in commercials, including one for Levi's directed by Bay. I was also on a Supercuts commercial and instead of having hair, I had snakes on top of my head like Medusa, the Greek mythology monster.

It was a good look.

I also got a credit as a stuntman in a film called *Agent Red* starring Dolph Lungdren, the guy who played Drago and fought

Stallone in *Rocky IV.* I was a submarine officer and when we got attacked and gassed by the enemy, we had to pass out. So my job was to fake fainting. It wasn't my greatest role.

I was aggressive in trying to build relationships in the film business because that seemed to be the best way to get regular work as an actor. Besides Mickey, I became friends with several other well-known actors, some of whom really surprised me because they seemed so unhappy and unfulfilled. Acting is such a fickle business. Unless you are a superstar, you are always nervous about the next opportunity. Many of those guys were worried about their future – if and when they might get their next job. They wondered if they were aging out of their careers. Their negativity amazed me. I'd tell them, "You guys have all the money and all the fame and you're still unhappy." Their lack of confidence was disturbing. If someone of their stature had so much uncertainty in their life, what did that mean for me?

I started having doubts about my future in acting.

But I kept at it for a while, although in terms of living my life, I was in a very wacky place. Until I was 40, I was doing some bouncing and working also as a doorman, but I never saved a penny. I bought Harley-Davidsons and cars, then stopped working and sold them to survive. I'd go back to work for six months, save some money and then be out of a job again.

I continued to pursue minor roles because that was the way to break into acting. Small roles would lead to bigger ones. I would go see many movies and focus on actors with minor roles. I knew I was as good, or better than them. I went to method acting school for two years and was thrilled when Robert De Niro spoke at our graduation. I figured I'd make a name for myself as a method actor and I was determined to do anything to make it happen.

My disjointed lifestyle and my determination to make acting work resulted in me becoming kind of desperate. I was frustrated that I could not get auditions for roles that seemed perfect for me, so I somehow developed a plan that seemed logical at the time but was truly idiotic. I started crashing other castings and pestering directors.

All my friends now are yogis, but back then, they were all actors. I would find out from one of them that auditions were scheduled for a certain time at Warner Bros., or Sony. I'd figure out a scam to get past the gate guards, or I would jump a fence and line up with the hopefuls. I also knew people who worked at studios so I would ask them if I could come for lunch and I'd get onto the movie lots that way. I got kicked out of auditions a few times, but it wasn't a very hostile thing. It was like, "You're not signed in" so I was escorted out. I was fine with that. You try, you get caught, you move on.

Not many opportunities came from that approach, however. It was not a productive way to gain attention. Anything I got came from the nightclubs, meeting people and them asking me if I wanted to do something. All my roles were small, kind of like throw-away roles as more of a favor to me than anything else. And I got the parts on my own, without an agent, just by knowing someone, knocking on doors or making phone calls.

I had worked hard to get into the industry, spending two years in school and paying for it by working long nights. I had built relationships and had done everything right. But I continued to be ignored and that led to desperation and obnoxious behavior that irritated the hell out of very powerful people. I would write a four-page letter about why I should get a role, walk in Jerry Bruckheimer's office and leave it on his desk. That simply is not done. I also burned bridges with Michael Bay because I started hounding him for jobs and he went out of his way to avoid me.

After *Armageddon*, I thought I was just about to start getting great parts and I had decided I was going to be an actor the rest of my life. They always say in show business, don't have a Plan B because if you have a Plan B, it will become Plan A. That business is too tough to deal with unless you are totally committed. And sure enough when I was 40, I didn't see a happy Hollywood ending in my future. And although I obviously had no way of knowing it at the time, yoga was about to become my plan B.

CHAPTER 8 - BIKING WITH STEVE MCQUEEN'S BIKE

Another connection I had with some of my film star friends was the motorcycle. I always loved Harley-Davidsons, which, of course, all badasses are supposed to love. So a couple of years after I moved to L.A., I bought one. At the time, it represented a sense of rebellion, a sense of freedom, a sense of power. It was kind of my image - if you want to make a grand entrance, a Harley is a spectacular way to do it. When I was working the crappy bars, it fit in perfectly - bouncer who kicks ass and rolls up to work on a monster bike that rattles the walls? Priceless.

But it also worked at the trendy bars, where the site and sound of arriving on a Harley while wearing a suit and tie was also quite a spectacle. The bike scene was huge in Los Angeles at the time. All the rock stars and movie stars were on motorcycles. All of them. Bikes had a storied history in L.A. They became a staple in Hollywood in 1953 when Marlon Brando starred in *The Wild One.* That influenced several generations of bikers and the motorcycle scene was thriving in the early '90s.

As you might expect, Mickey Rourke was a biker and I spent time riding with him. But the most amazing experience was riding with Chad McQueen, the son of the late Steve McQueen. I was a Steve McQueen freak. He was the essence of cool and when I was growing up, every young male wanted to be just like him. His movies were great - *The Cincinnati Kid, The Magnificent Seven, The Thomas Crown Affair, Papillon, Bullitt, The Getaway, The Towering*

Inferno, The Sand Pebbles and *The Great St. Louis Bank Robbery*. But his greatest motorcycle scene – and one of the best ever – was in *The Great Escape*, when he tried to get away from German soldiers, who eventually caught him. You can still see that seven-minute scene on YouTube. McQueen was a collector of rare motorbikes and one of them sold at an auction in 2015 for $775,000. When Chad McQueen rode with us, he'd be on one of his dad's bikes.

I also met and hung out with few of the Hells Angels. I really liked and could relate to those guys, but although the opportunity was there, I never really considered joining the group for the long haul. In the past, I had not been much interested in being a leader; I was much more comfortable being a lone wolf. Still am today. And after my experience with Larry the drug dealer, my days of being a follower were over.

But I did enjoy riding with them. You're typically not allowed to ride with the Hells Angels unless you've earned their colors, but they were friends of mine and they would let me ride with them on occasion – not officially, but with one or two of them. I know they have a violent reputation, but bikers for the most part as some of the best people you will ever meet. If you ever need back up or even more, bikers are there, 24/7. I've found that Marines and bikers share the same DNA.

I managed to get into more trouble – or put myself in danger of getting into more trouble – when I was alone rather than riding with them. One of my jobs was at another trendy club named

Stringfellows, which was at the corner of Rodeo Drive and Wilshire Boulevard in Beverly Hills. I was head of VIP security at the time but that didn't prevent me from becoming, as far as I know, the only person in history to throw a champagne bottle in the air and shoot it with a 9 mm pistol on top of a building on Rodeo Drive.

After we closed one night, we went to the roof to drink some champagne and for some reason, I decided it would be entertaining to throw the bottle in the air and shoot it.

Great idea in Beverly Hills, where there's no crime.

Within minutes, the cops showed up and said they'd received reports of gunshots. I talked to them and said we had heard nothing but they were free to come in and check the place out. Since I was head of security, they were satisfied and left. It was an example of how I still had moments of craziness – like I did in the Marines two decades earlier when I used the M-16 to shoot phone booths. It seems if you owned a Harley, you had a streak of defiance and mine came out periodically.

The interesting part of that period was that I had already discovered yoga so I was still making the transition from short fuse to yogi. It was a gradual process. My yoga friends weren't quite sure what to think of me. When I attended classes, I strapped a yoga mat to my back and when I arrived on the Harley, everyone knew it because the entire place would shake. Yoga and biking provided an interesting contrast in my life and I knew it was kind of crazy. I made up a saying about myself that I would use a lot in the next few years.

I had one foot in the dark and one foot in the light.

* * *

From 1991 to 2000, the Harley was my only means of transportation. It took me everywhere, rain or shine. I rode it to work, rode it to acting school, rode it to auditions, rode it to yoga class, rode it with friends and rode it to meet girls. I had only a few problems, some far worse than others.

In '97, I was hired by hotel magnate himself, Ian Schrager, who owned the famous Mondrian Hotel on Sunset Blvd. in the middle of West Hollywood. The Mondrian, home of the Skybar lounge, was a luxury boutique hotel. It was a top-notch, celebrity-central, Hollywood-elite type of thing. I was hired as the lobby manager so I would walk around in a suit in the lobby greeting all the guests, the producers and directors who I knew from my nightclub days. It was a good job with a good future if I had wanted it.

But as it turned out, I didn't. I had it for about three months, then crashed my motorcycle, broke my leg and arm. I was living in a garage apartment at the very top of the Hollywood Hills above Sunset Blvd. I could not ride the bike so I was trapped like a rat for about six weeks and that was as long as I could go without losing my patience, which I did. My arm and leg were about three quarters of the way healed, but I could wait no longer so I took a butcher knife and sawed both casts off.

I still needed money, of course, and I do have a very high threshold of pain. So I walked around the hotel with my arm looking like a toothpick and limping on my broken leg. But I had no interest in the job. What little motivation I had anyway was soon lost and they got tired of watching me sneak out back to smoke cigars. So they fired me and that was just fine with me. The calm of yoga was still having a hard time kicking in, but certain events hardly helped.

For instance, having my Harley stolen twice. The first time was in 1995 and I remember crying like a baby because I didn't have any insurance on it. I was living in Venice and lying on the sofa one Saturday afternoon watching North Carolina playing Florida State in basketball. I heard a motorcycle start but there were many motorcycles in the neighborhood. Then I heard it burn out and I knew it was mine. But by the time I got my gun and sprinted downstairs, it was gone. I went back to watching the game again but I was devastated. Not only was my bike gone, Carolina was down 20 points. However, as in life, the Tar Heels had an amazing comeback and won the game. The whole time, I was crying my eyes out. So there I was, happy my team was winning, but bawling. Some of the tears were because of the great comeback, and some were because without my bike I felt I was doomed.

For three years, I had to ride the city bus, which I called "the loser cruiser." And then, amazingly, I got a call from the police and they said they had found the bike. I went to the station, but the one they had was a full-blown chopper. It wasn't mine. The cop told me the VIN on the transmission was the same and the thieves must have torn it down and replaced it with a new frame. He looked at me, winked and said, “This is your bike, isn’t it?” I said, “Yeah, that’s my fucking bike.” So they gave it to me.

The second time it got stolen, I had insurance because I had learned my lesson. I called the insurance company and reported it. They were going to send me a check for $20,000 but then the craziest thing happened. I went to see my girlfriend and she lived in a big complex with an indoor parking garage. I tried to get in the front door of the complex to get to her apartment but it wouldn’t open. The garage gate door did, however, because a guy was pulling out. So I went in that way. I was walking to the elevator and out of the corner of my eye, I saw something sticking out behind the dumpster. I checked it out and there’s my motorcycle. I found it myself.

The last problem ended my Harley days. In 2010 I was riding across an intersection and a guy ran a stoplight and hit me. My bike was torn in half, the impact flipped me through the air and I was an inch away from being killed. His fender nipped the front of my shinbone and the cop said if he’d hit me an inch back I would have lost my leg. I went flying through the air, through two lanes of traffic and landed on my left butt and left shoulder. I was lying there and here’s the funny part. I was trying to get up but I couldn’t move. A cab driver who looked and sounded to me as though he may have been from India was standing over me and kept saying, “Don’t move, I think you’re dead.” I smiled a painful smile but his words did bother me a bit at the time.

I did have a horrible and painful hip contusion which meant I couldn't walk for a month. But everything else healed and I was fine. That was August 2010 and my daughter was born in October so I decided it was best not to get another bike. I still love Harleys, however, and some day, I'll be cruising the PCH again.

CHAPTER 9 - BODYGUARD FOR THE RICH AND FAMOUS

While I was working as a doorman and pursuing the actor angle, I picked up a few jobs as a celebrity bodyguard and forgot about the idea of being a cop. The only time I really thought about it seriously was in 1991 when it was still Plan B. But as I was considering whether or not I wanted to apply to the LAPD, the Rodney King tape was released and four white officers were charged with using excessive force in apprehending King, who was on parole for a previous robbery conviction. The officers were later acquitted in L.A. of charges against them, but then federal charges were filed and two of them had to serve time in jail.

For me, the result of the Rodney King incident was that it ended any thoughts I had of being Mel Gibson in *Lethal Weapon.* The department instituted a program that focused on hiring minorities and there was a hiring freeze for white men so I continued working as a bouncer.

I still had thoughts of being a celebrity bodyguard. I had read that *Playboy* article in 1980 when I was stationed in South Carolina and it seemed so glamorous:

Gavin de Becker! Security for the stars!

In 1995, I was working as head of VIP security for the House of Blues when it opened. It was the "in" place for the moment and everyone from Dan Aykroyd to Bruce Springsteen came in. On opening night, I recognized de Becker and introduced myself. Later, I was talking to one of the guys with him and I told him I had read the *Playboy* article when I was in the Marines and I always considered working for the company. The guy told me to come by the office and apply for a job, which I did – on my Harley, of course. But I found out the job was very low-paying. At the time I could make as much as $1,000 a night three nights a week. That comes out to $150,000 a year and Gavin wasn't even close to that.

I discovered, however, there was another way to be a celebrity bodyguard. We always had celebrities at the clubs where I worked, so I began giving them my phone number to let them know I was available. I also asked them to recommend me to anyone who might be looking for a bodyguard, and that's how I got to work for Pam Anderson, Arsenio Hall, Warren Beatty, Marlon Brando and many others. Amazingly, I even got a one-day job working security for the Elizabeth Taylor.

Although there were never any problems on those jobs, I did find out that celebrities can do some pretty unusual things. I will, of course, keep those to myself for a variety of reasons, not the least of which would be to avoid lawsuits.

As I continued to meet stars, I became more confident and aggressive. That led to several jobs working for Sylvester Stallone. I met him in an elevator at a club going down to the valet on Rodeo Drive in Beverly Hills. I knew he had a bodyguard named Gary, who was a big giant guy. Stallone was always getting into trouble because people were so aggressive around him. Everyone wanted to out-Rambo Rambo or out-Rocky Rocky. I remember once he got sued because he got into a fight with a guy I think was the paparazzi and I'd heard he'd lost a lawsuit and it cost him big money. I thought to myself that if he had a good bodyguard, trouble could be kept away from him.

When I met him, I told him I was interested and he said Gary was his head of security. I told him I knew Gary and Gary was the one who suggested I make the pitch. I decided the best approach was to be bold, but I was surprised when it worked so perfectly. "Yeah," he said with that Rocky accent, "I could probably use some extra help." I offered to drive him home on the spot and he said, "Ambitious, huh? I like that." So I drove him home and I got a taxi back to my place. I started getting calls from Gary to work at events Stallone was attending, so it was a good move on my part.

Another highlight was the experience with Elizabeth Taylor. She is a legend, one of the most famous people in the history of film, so it was an honor to be in her detail. She came to a jewelry store for a release party on a diamond and high-end jewels on Rodeo Drive and the guy in charge said, "I want you to stand two feet from Ms. Taylor and just stand over her shoulder." So I stood there looking real hard and menacing and professional with the little earphone plugged in my ear. I never got to talk to her, but I was close by all day. She came across as a very classy lady and was genuinely kind to people and not full of herself.

Overall, my bodyguard experiences were tame. You would think there would be problems and you'd have to get into fights, but I didn't. It was really so simple. You would be assigned to a person and walked several feet behind him or her. You did the whole thing with the earpiece in your ear. It was more for show than anything else. The stars like to have handsome former military men looking razor sharp watching over them yet never quite getting in their way, a ghost if you will. There was little or no communication with the celebrities. Most of the ones I worked for wouldn't even know my name if they saw me.

The bodyguard thing did not last long because I decided I had bigger fish to fry. However, I did like the fact that I had achieved a goal - checked a box on my bucket list. It's something I had set out to do years before and to this day when I make up my mind to do something I hardly ever fail.

Although the job allowed me to be close to the rich and famous, it was not challenging - certainly nothing like acting. I found that it took very little talent to be a great bodyguard. And for me, it was easy to get to the top level of the profession with little effort. I think it was also proof that whoever wrote that we tend to be good at what we have the capacity to be good at was exactly right. We gravitate to what we can do very well. We're all a genius in something and I tend to be a genius at certain things. In the military, I was great at it when I chose to be. Sports I was always good and sometimes great. What I do now, teaching yoga, I'm great at. Security stuff I was great at, police work I could've been good at it if I had kept my criminal tendencies under control.

But I got to the point where I did not like the bodyguard thing. It bored me and I could do better, although there was one element that I liked. When I walked out a door with a client and the fans and paparazzi went wild, I was in my element. Had I become a movie star, I would have been very comfortable with fame.

CHAPTER 10 - HALF-ASSED YOGA

My infatuation with body building began when I was in high school and read the article about Casey Viator, who was Mr. America at age 19. When Kyle McKinley, who had graduated the year before me, visited my class in high school and had put on 30 pounds of muscle, I figured one of the benefits of the military would be a free place to train and that was exciting.

When I was assigned to the Marine Corps Air Station at Cherry Point, North Carolina, as an MP, I quickly found the gym and it became a refuge for me. I was consumed with the way I could train and change my body. Getting stronger also helped a lot when I was a bouncer at cowboy, redneck and biker bars that surrounded the base in the coastal towns of North Carolina.

After a few years of living in California, I joined the original Gold's Gym in Venice, which is also known as "the Mecca of bodybuilding." It became famous when it was featured in the 1977 Arnold Schwarzenegger movie *Pumping Iron* and has been referred to as "a landmark in the cult of bodybuilding." It's a place where people from all over the world, even Olympic champions, come to work out. In the bodybuilding culture, it's Harvard and I was after my strength and conditioning PhD.

Ironically, it's where I discovered yoga, but only because I did something stupid. I was at UCLA with some friends and we were in the gym where there were two ropes side by side tied to rafters. I told them how I had trained on ropes in the Marines and how badass I was at climbing them. When they doubted me, I had to prove it. The problem was that I was 22 in the Marines and 35 at UCLA, so I managed to tear my rotator cuff climbing the two ropes with one hand on each rope and not using my legs. That kept me off the weights for a few weeks.

I still worked out at Gold's but was limited with my shoulder injury. One day, I was walking around the place, which is huge, and I went by a room where there were a gaggle of women in a yoga class. I didn't have any idea what the hell they were doing but since the room was full of well-shaped, good-looking women in what I learned later was the down dog pose, I was all in. I looked at the schedule for the next day, saw a listing for "Hatha Yoga, level 1," and I signed up. Little did I know at that moment I would not only be hooked on it immediately, but that it also would become a passion and a profession. At first blush, I thought it would at the least be a chance to do some easy stretching and perhaps get lucky with one of the perfectly-shaped females. The whole enlightenment thing was something at the time I couldn't fathom. But like I now always say: Be careful because the practice will take over your life. It did mine.

Yoga did not result in major changes right away, however. I was still in that period of being a bouncer, doorman, bodyguard, actor and beach bum working on my tan. After a couple of classes, I was drawn to yoga, but I was years away from having the thought that it could be a fulltime job.

At the time, I was still living a ragged and carefree lifestyle.

There was nothing spiritual or disciplined about my approach to life other then my physical pursuits. I was a dreamer of bigger things to come and the thought of working a 9-to-5 sounded like death. It still does. But despite having very little money, I had no concerns. In fact, I reveled in my poverty. For a time, I even challenged myself to live on $5 a day.

I was getting a small amount of money from my movie and commercial work. Even though I wasn't in the final cut of *The Rock*, I'd still get residual checks of about $125 every quarter. Sometimes, they'd start running an old commercial I had done and a check for $600 would show up. I was also collecting unemployment and then when things got really tight, I'd take a couple of bouncing jobs, put the money in my account and then not find work again for a couple of months.

* * *

Despite that lifestyle, I stayed in great shape. I lived at the top of Hollywood Hills with a friend who let me live in a garage apartment when I had the money for rent, but also would let me sleep in a small room that wasn't much bigger than a van when I was broke. I lived in that area off and on for three years and shared the space with my 100-pound Labrador Retriever, who I named Mr. R, and a big fat rat I called Willard that was the size of a kitten. One night around 2 a.m., Willard ambushed me, leaping off the dryer in the garage and onto my chest. Scared the hell out of me – and then and there we had a fight to the finish, I pummeled him with a broom then scooped him up. He was wiggling and trying to bite me so I hurled him down the high cliff overlooking Sunset Blvd.

Willard never came back.

In those early days of learning and practicing yoga, I didn't let anything interfere with my yoga class schedule. From the top of Hollywood Hills overlooking the House of Blues, it took me 30 minutes to walk down the hill to catch a bus to UCLA on Sunset Boulevard. I would change buses at UCLA and get on one to Santa Monica and I would practice yoga for two hours. Then I'd take a bus back to UCLA, transfer to a Hollywood bus, and when I got to my stop on Sunset, I would have a 40-minute climb to my place. I did that every day for a year and I never had much money. But I loved it, I looked at it as kind of like Spartan training.

I thought at the time that I was not advancing in my life, but I learned in my tough times everything you do, every triumph you have, leads you to somewhere greater. Those years, like my childhood, are years I would not exchange for anything because they have made my mind and body damn near indestructible.

Reality eventually beckons, however. Looking back, even though I had avoided a dishonorable discharge in the Marines, and even though I had survived the relationship with a drug dealer, and even though it had been years since I had worms in my stools from working on the Pughs' pig farm, it felt like my life was the same as it had always been - a lifelong struggle and I was behind where I thought I should have been. Funny thing is that it never got me down. Somewhere along the way, I became the eternal optimist. Still am.

Besides continuing to practice yoga, I was in the best shape of my life because of where I lived and how I got there. I created a competition for myself. When I got home from yoga each day, instead of walking up the hill 40 minutes, I ran up the hill. It was like Marine training. I was in better shape than I was at 20 years old and in the military, despite my diet, which was a result of my not being responsible enough to keep a fulltime job.

For breakfast, I would walk down the hills to McDonald's and they would have a special of two Egg McMuffins for the price of one. I would eat one for breakfast, take the egg out of the second one and save it. I'd get a can of tuna fish at the 99-cent store and for lunch I would put the tuna fish on one half of the bread. For dinner, I'd eat the other half of the bread and the leftover egg. That would be all I had. I was 38 years old. It wasn't the greatest diet, but I was certainly lean.

I was still not working a real job, but I was chasing auditions, so there was quite a contrast in my life. I loved the physical part of running up Hollywood Hills and training but as far as working a regular job, not so much. Despite that, I don't remember ever being worried. I had no money, but I had freedom and I told myself everything was great. Amazingly, I was pretty happy.

* * *

Stanton was a friend from South Carolina who had moved to L.A. and had become very successful and very wealthy. He owned the house I lived in and was always very kind and supportive toward me. But one day, I was walking down the hill and he was driving by in his Mercedes convertible and stopped when he saw me.

"What am I going to do with you?" he said, and shook his head. I had been there for several years and had little money, no regular job, no schedule and no life plan.

Turned out, I needed Stan's disgust because I took it as a challenge to find the answer. Despite deluding myself into thinking everything was great, I knew in the back of my mind that I needed to do something. I was still pursuing acting roles, but nothing had happened to make me optimistic. I was getting too old to apply at LAPD as a fallback position and I no longer liked bodyguard work. I was tired of bouncing and nightclubs, even though I continued working for them when I needed money. And although I had a passing thought that I might do something in yoga, it was only a glimmer in the back of my mind.

I owed Stan some money, so I got a nightclub job briefly, made a bunch of money and got my own place. By that time I had been to probably 300 yoga classes and I had decided that I knew as much or more than some of the instructors I had. I also had met Bryan Kest, who became one of the most influential people in my life. Bryan is one of the top yoga instructors in the world and someone who had an infinitely different approach to the age-old practice than most.

Bryan was a radical teacher, a rebel on the American yoga scene. He was the first teacher I had taken a class from that was very physical with none of the psychobabble, pseudo-religion bullshit. And with my dedication to weight training and body building, the physical part was what I was after at that time.

I had met a friend in a yoga class and I told her that I liked yoga, but I wanted something more strenuous. She told me I should try Bryan's class because it was very different, so I did.

I went to the first class and she was right. He was shouting out commands, cursing, had long hair and seemed like yoga's version of a punk rocker –rebellious and unconventional. He'd walk around the class and if someone was distracted or not paying attention he'd say, "Don't bring your shit into yoga and turn your yoga into shit." But he did it in a humorous way. I loved it.

Bryan invented Power Yoga, which is a much more active, physically-demanding type of yoga, but it was closely modeled on the *Ashtanga* method, which Bryan learned while studying in India. Right away, I said to myself that I get this guy. This is more like it. Bryan is the one who took my interest level up a notch.

For the first few years of yoga, I didn't think about teaching because I just enjoyed the classes. I was still working at clubs at night, but I never really liked the late scene. I kept doing it because the money was good and I had nothing else. But after going through a few of Bryan's classes, I started thinking I might be able to teach. So I went to Bryan and asked him his opinion. His response was typical Bryan – over the top.

"I've told two people this in my life and one is Seane Corn," he said and got my attention. In the yoga world, Corn was a superstar. "You should teach yoga." For me, it was like Bill Belichick going up to a third string punter and saying, "I think you'd be a good coach." I was ecstatic, but I had no idea how to do it. So I asked Bryan if I needed teacher training and, being very anti-establishment, he just erupted.

"You don't need any goddamn teacher training," he yelled. "Do you feel like you can teach yoga?" I said I could. I told him that when I started yoga, I got it immediately. I told him that I totally understood it and I could teach it tomorrow. I felt it inherently in my bones from being an athlete my whole life. I knew anatomically how to move my body the way yoga did. I may not be able to do every move because of my size, more linebacker than hippie, but I understood the technical part of it, the science of it and the theory of it. And so I said "I can teach this stuff tomorrow."

"Well, then get a space and start teaching," he said, making it sound simple. He told me he started when he found a dance studio and it wasn't being used and asked the owner if he could teach yoga. The guy said he would charge $50 an hour for the space. So he would pay the guy $50 an hour but he'd make many times that because another of his innovations is donation-based fees. He suggests a certain amount, but people can pay more or less than that. *LA Weekly*, the alternative newspaper in L.A., put it this way: "Kest pioneered 'suggested donation' yoga in L.A., effectively removing the class divide that previously rendered wealthy

Angelenos toned and superior, and the poor ones soft and anxious. It's sweat-soaked wisdom in a room packed with Lycra and longing. In the illustrious words of Kest himself: "It's like a dance class but without the bulimia."

* * *

Although I appreciated Bryan's optimism, I felt the same way I had when I wanted to be an actor. I thought I had the talent to act, but wanted the benefit of training so I could understand the technique. The same was true of yoga. I felt like I had the talent to teach right away, but I wanted the technique and verbalization to give me confidence. So I went to the greatest teacher training in the world, which was Yoga Works and got my training from Matty Ezraty, Lisa Wofford and later Annie Carpenter, among many others.

When I moved away from the garage apartment, I stayed in Hollywood and moved next door to an Episcopal church. When I first got there, I went inside because I wanted to find a good place to meditate. I wanted a quiet place to sit and it looked very peaceful. It had been built in the 1930s and there was a small building behind the church. I looked in the window and there was a hardwood floor and I figured 50 or 60 people would fit in that room easily. So I decided to teach yoga like Bryan did.

I was concerned, however, because I thought there was no way a Christian church was going to let me teach a Hindu practice. Then I started thinking about it and I remembered Episcopalians are very liberal. They allow priests to marry and divorce, they allow women to be priests and they have long accepted gays and lesbians. They even have clergy who are openly gay.

So I knocked on the pastor's door and asked him about the space. He said it was a community room and that it was used for meetings and events. It was also a polling place for the elections. I asked if it would be possible to rent it when nothing else was scheduled and he said no problem. He charged me $25 an hour, which meant the overhead was minimal.

I was getting excited about the possibilities and quickly made flyers advertising the "Yoga Warrior." Right above the church there was this great hiking trail called Runyon Canyon. All the beautiful people – actresses, writers, celebrities, models and everyone in the industry – hiked that trail. It is a very athletic trail. So I handed out flyers with donation-based yoga on it and did it for about two weeks.

In the first class there were about 20 people there and I was encouraged. After we finished, several people came up to me and said it was the best yoga class they'd ever had. They said no one has been able to teach like me, which was funny because I had just copied what I learned in another class I had been in the day before. It was like muscle memory and I just blurted it out. I had graduated from method acting school so I figured I was kind of like Robert De Niro or Marlon Brando. I had the same kind of technique. Before I went to acting school, I was nervous speaking in front of crowds. But when you are acting and you're doing these monologues in front of the producers, directors, other actors and the crew, you quickly lose your anxiety. I even did a couple of live plays, so by the time I started teaching yoga, I was comfortable as a public speaker and a performer. It was a natural progression of going from acting to teaching yoga.

Word spread quickly after the first class. In my second class, there were 30, and in the next class, 40. That's where I honed my skills; it was my apprenticeship.

At that point, I was still bouncing and being a doorman and not making very much as a yoga teacher and there were times when my job and my emerging passion conflicted. One night I was working as a doorman at a club and a guy kept trying to get in when I told him there was no room. Finally we got into a fight and the guy could take care of himself. It was very physical and both of us ended up being pretty beat up. The fight was broken up and he left. I was trying to get myself straightened up, picking up my clipboard, adjusting my tie and this girl was at the front of the line talking, but I was preoccupied and not listening. I thought she was demanding to get into the club so I finally said, "Just give me a goddamn minute" because I'm all freaked out about the fight. Finally, I snapped at her and said, "Now what the fuck do you want?" And she said, "I just wanted to say hi. I'm in your yoga class on Saturdays." That's when I would tell my friends that I had one foot in the light and one foot in the dark. At nighttime I'm choking people and throwing them out the back door and I'm teaching yoga in the morning. It was quite the dichotomy.

As I kept teaching, however, and word spread, my income increased to the point where I could teach fulltime and leave the world of nightclubs. Looking back, it actually happened pretty quickly. I went from three nights of bouncing to two, then to one and then suddenly, I wasn't working in clubs anymore and I was teaching.

Eventually, however, the Episcopal church began having more events in that room and sometimes they would rent it out for a month. I couldn't put out a regular schedule so I stopped the classes. By that time I had two years of teaching under my belt and I was still practicing under Bryan because I considered him to be my mentor. He knew I had been teaching for a couple of years but after I lost the church space, I talked to him and he said it wasn't as bad as it seemed. He had decided to open a second studio. He said he had 150 people in his first studio and he couldn't teach them all. The new place was only two blocks away and he could give me a full schedule.

It was fortunate timing. We opened the studio on Second Street in downtown Santa Monica and I had a job.

35 years of strength - conditioning training with yoga are the mainstays of my physical and emotional life. I'm not sure where I'd be without them.

Keeping a watchful eye on a room full of yoga students.

Teaching seated forward fold using blocks.

Teaching a yoga workshop

A playful moment with mentor, friend, and Udaya CEO Yariv Lerner, who to his credit thinks all things are possible.

"Rudy! I remember when he started coming to my classes years ago; he was humble and dedicated, strong and steady. Rudy is a practitioner - and in his case the alchemy of yoga has worked its magic! Yoga has melted Rudy's toughness and sweetened his ways."

Annie Carpenter
Yoga Teacher
Creator of the Smart Flow Yoga Training

"Rudy's say-it-like-it-is approach is refreshing, humorous, and heartfelt. Whether he's telling a story, teaching a yoga class, or simply engaging you in friendly conversation, you'll be seduced by his wit and charm."

Jules Mitchell
MS, Yoga Teacher, Yoga Educator

CHAPTER 11 - ACTING SUCKS

When I first started teaching Yoga, I had not yet given up on the acting career. I still had to pay the bills so I continued bouncing in clubs. As I built my reputation as a yoga teacher, Bryan increased the number of classes I taught and eventually I was able to teach fulltime. In retrospect it happened quickly - a couple of years. At the time, however, it was a gradual process that enabled me to develop my philosophy and approach to the practice.

My dream of being a fulltime actor finally crashed around 2002 when two very irritating things happened. I had worn directors and producers out with my obnoxious aggressiveness, but my approach also demonstrated desire. Plus I was desperate. When I was slammed twice in a short period, however, I knew it was time to move on in my life.

I had read the book *We Were Soldiers Once . . . And Young,* which was set during the Vietnam war and ran 432 pages. I was particularly moved by one scene where a soldier is holding another soldier who is dying and the last thing the guy says is "Tell my wife I love her." And then he dies. When I read it, I thought it would be a great movie scene. In acting classes, we were taught to always think creatively while we were reading or watching something and I imagined the book characters as characters in a movie.

Six months after I read the book, I heard the movie *We Were Soldiers,* which was based on the book and was starring Mel Gibson, was being made. It was directed by Randall Wallace, who wrote the script for Braveheart, and I was determined to get a role in it since I had just read the book. A friend of mine who worked for a big talent agency was able to get the script and he gave me a copy to read.

I had been very diligent about reading scripts. I always looked for small roles because I was realistic enough to know those were the only ones I could get. I also thought that if I could get several roles and get some notice, it could lead to bigger roles.

The *We Were Soldiers* script was only 90 pages long, but the part I had picked out was in it. The movie scene duplicates what is in the book. A wounded soldier is being held by a buddy. The camera pans into a close-up of a trembling hand and the soldier says, "Tell my wife I love her."

I was thrilled. The book was 432 pages. The scene that I thought was perfect for me – a small, but dramatic role – made it into the 90-page script. This was destiny. The role was meant to be for me. I knew it.

I found out who was doing the casting and I wrote a letter to Wallace. I asked Michael Bay if he could get me a meeting with Wallace and Michael gave me the phone number of several people and said they might be able to help. But no one returned my calls. I wrote two letters, and heard nothing back. So I sent flowers to the agency, hoping they would find the right person.

I found out the casting was being held in the San Fernando Valley, which is in the northern part of L.A. and about an hour drive, and I hopped on the Harley and headed out. When I got there,

I managed to find the right office and introduced myself to one of the assistants. She wrote down my name and looked at it for several seconds like she had seen it before. "Did you send me flowers last week?" she asked. Smiling, I said yes. The long shot had paid off.

I read for the part, but several months went by and I heard nothing. One night I was at the movies and saw a preview that *We Were Soldiers* was coming out in March. Obviously I did not get the part.

Trailers are only two minutes long, but they contain the most powerful stuff from the movie. About halfway through, the wounded soldier and his buddy appear and my line is uttered by another man: "Tell my wife I love her."

I had conflicting emotions. One was pride. Out of 432 pages, I had discovered the character long before a movie was planned. The scene not only made the movie, but was also in the trailer. That led to other emotions – disappointment, frustration, anger. That role should have been mine.

I ran into someone later who had worked in the movie and he said they shot the scene in Georgia so they just hired someone local for that role. They didn't have to fly anyone out there and put them up in a hotel, so they saved money.

About the same time, I thought something positive was going to happen. I had an audition for *The Matrix Reloaded*, the second film in the *Matrix* series, and the directors actually had me read for the part three times. Not only did I not get it, but a friend of mine was hired instead.

That did it for me. I said fuck it.

I had really wanted the role in *We Were Soldiers*, as small as it was, because I felt that since I had picked it out, I had a good feel for what worked on the screen. I felt that I understood the artistry of what made a good scene and I felt I had talent to act. Then to get so close to being in the *Matrix* movie was maddening. Those two things happened very close to each other and I just couldn't handle it. They drove me right out of the business.

* * *

My career as an actor was a modest one and I did make some mistakes with my approach. But I also gave it everything I had. I pursued every role, read hundreds of scripts, wrote letters and made phone calls. I was serious about learning the craft, which is why I went to acting school for two years, footing the expensive bill with my bouncing jobs at night.

Ironically, acting classes helped me enormously as a yoga teacher. When I first went to acting school, I wasn't comfortable as a public speaker. I was unsure of myself and had no confidence. But when you act, you have to do scenes over and over. When you speak, everyone is watching and listening – the other actors, the producer, director, crew. Your lines are sometimes very long, and you have to memorize them. After a short time in acting school, I became more sure of myself. So when I began teaching yoga, I did not have stage fright. I was comfortable right away.

To be successful in this business, you have to be a little bit of the showman and a little bit of a ham, a little bit of a know-it-all and I happen to have all those things in spades. So my development was quick and almost spontaneous.

The combination of my training as an actor and my success as a yoga instructor led to a different sort of acting opportunity. Yariv Lerner began attending my classes several years ago and when I got to know him a little, I discovered he was the CEO of Udaya Entertainment. Yariv, who was once a professional beach volleyball player, was so enthusiastic about the way I taught that he suggested that we should go into business.

Yariv comes from an entertainment family; his father Avi has produced more than 350 films including all of the *Expendables* movies, the *Rambo* movies, *Conan the Barbarian* and many more. Yariv has been on film sets all his life, so he drew upon his experiences and produced *Yoga Warrior 365 with Rudy Mettia*, a set of 12 CDs and a bonus CD that captures my approach to teaching yoga.

At first, Yariv and I discussed opening a brick-and-mortar yoga center, but instead, we have supplemented the classes I already teach at Power Yoga with an online business. Making the CDs was our first step and although nothing could be cooler than having your own CD set, the experience of doing it was pretty amazing.

Yariv has this great studio in Sofia, Bulgaria, and it has quite a history. The facility was once a communist propaganda center and although it is bland inside the building – like you would expect something from the former Soviet Union to be – traveling halfway across the world to make a yoga DVD was a remarkable experience. We shot the DVD in a room that looked like a replica of the Roman Coliseum, so it is a unique setting you won't find anywhere else.

We now go to Bulgaria, where it is far less expensive to make a DVD because of lower labor costs, twice a year and we invite students to make the trip with us. They pay for their own plane ticket but we give them a hotel and give them food and transportation. It's like a big giant yoga retreat.

* * *

Bryan Kest taught me that radical is good and over the years, I've developed a philosophy that is unique to me. I had an innate ability to understand yoga, which Bryan reinforced when he told me that I was one of only two of his students at the time that he thought should teach yoga. The other was Seane Corn, an international superstar.

Although I was thrilled with Bryan's encouragement, I had the same philosophy about teaching that I had about acting. Even though I thought I had the ability to act, I wanted validation and I wanted to know the craft behind it. So I went to acting school. When I was preparing to teach yoga, I knew I wanted to take a teacher training course to study technique and enhance my natural ability. Of course, I also went for the validation and to learn the verbiage and art to each posture.

When I began classes, what I thought would happen did, in fact, happen. The trainers would show the class a pose or a technique and I'd think to myself, "Oh hell, I know that."

It's been said that yoga is more about remembering, than learning what the body already knows. Yoga teacher training gave me the words to articulate what my body already knew. I invested 200 hours to get my Level 1 certification and then went on to take more than 500 hours of training that I needed to obtain my advanced certification. I think training courses are important for the majority of people, but for me they simply reinforced the talent and ability I already had. I believe I'm a teacher at heart, so whether I am teaching yoga, strength and conditioning or how to use firearms, I employ the same techniques. Teaching is teaching, plain and simple, if you have the heart and dedication to succeed at it.

* * *

I had taken some time off to concentrate on training, but when I started having classes at the Episcopal church, my approach was a combination of what I had learned from Bryan, what I had learned from teacher training and my own ideas on how I wanted to approach it. I like to say that anytime you start doing something, there are three stages to it. The first stage is you imitate, then you integrate and then you innovate. In the last few years I have trained many yoga instructors and when they start teaching, they copy me at first, just as I had copied my teachers. Then when they are comfortable in their own skin, they find their own voice and become their own person. The transformations my students go through is a very fulfilling part of my work.

Much of my confidence is from being an athlete my whole life. I know anatomically how to move my body the way yoga requires. I may not be able to do all the yoga moves because of my structure, shape and injuries, but I understand the technicality of it, the science of it and the theory of it.

Everybody is a genius at something and I think I'm a genius in the knowledge of the physical body. I know exactly how to work it and I can articulate that knowledge. I tell all the hopeful yoga teachers that I don't care what they know. I don't care if they know the ancient language of Sanskrit. You can speak all the Sanskrit words beautifully, all the sutras and scriptures and mantras and mudras. You can know all the hundreds of thousands of pages of yoga history because it's more than 5,000 years old and one of the oldest civilizations in the world. All knowledge helps, but what you have to be able to do is guide the students and provide them with an uplifting and fulfilling experience.

That's part of what makes yoga teachers so revered. They provide a beneficial experience for students, who then feel a bond with the teacher who led them. Students can get so attached to a teacher that they refuse to go another teacher. I have students like that. If I take a class off because of traveling, not feeling well or whatever, students will come in and say, "He's not here?" Some may have driven an hour, but they won't stay for the substitute. I used to be the same way. If I went to the studio and the teacher I liked wasn't there, I would not stay.

* * *

After five years of yoga and training I wasn't nearly as serious philosophically as many teachers might be. Bryan was a big proponent of never using Sanskrit because he thought it would intimidate and lessen the appeal of yoga to the masses. I've picked up some Sanskrit now because I'm in the business and I read. I know the words, but I'm nowhere near being a scholar. I believe that some teachers hide their shortcomings as tacticians by trying to show everyone their brilliance in Sanskrit. The greatest Asana teachers I know, however, do not believe that their knowledge of Sanskrit makes them more effective. I'm that way. My technique is rock solid, and no one cares that I didn't master the language. I know enough to get by. I read it and pay attention to it. But I know people who go to college to get their advanced degrees in Sanskrit. It just so happens that some of those people can't teach worth a damn.

The thing that makes yoga special is doing it with the right state of mind. My job as a teacher is to lead and inspire without trying to preach or convert. Yoga doesn't have to be mystical. It's not about religion. Yes, yoga is a Hindu practice, but it's more of a philosophy. You can be Jewish, Catholic, or any other religion and practice yoga. Hell, it may even make you better at Judaism, Christianity or Hinduism.

In the South, the heart of the Bible Belt where I was raised, they sometimes avoid using Hindu names. For example, the Virabhadrasana, Warrior Two posture may look similar to Jesus on the cross, so a Christian teacher may call it 'the cross pose." I'm good with that because getting people into yoga is my only concern.

In the South, instead of chanting, you may sing hallelujah. I told my sister in North Carolina I was teaching yoga and she said, "You know you're going to hell for praying to Buddha."

I said, "Number one, Buddha is not Hindu, he's Buddhist. And number two, I'm not praying to anybody, I'm just teaching physical asana and meditation."

There's even a scripture, Psalm 46:10, where it's written, "Be still and know that I am God." If that's not a call to meditate, I don't know what is.

Jesus would be down with that. I'm sure of it.

CHAPTER 12 - PUMPING THE BODY . . . AND THE MIND

The greatest feeling you can get in a gym, or the most satisfying feeling you can get in a gym is the pump. Let's say you train your biceps. Blood is rushing into your muscles and that would be called a pump. Your muscles get a really tight feeling like your skin is going to explode any minute. And it's really tight. It's like somebody blowing air into your muscle. It just blows up and it feels different. It feels fantastic. It's as satisfying to me as coming is, as having sex with a woman and coming. Can you believe how much I'm in heaven? I'm like getting the feeling of coming in the gym and I'm getting the feeling of coming at home. I'm getting the feeling of coming backstage when I pump up. When I pose out in front of 5,000 people, I get the same feeling so I'm coming day and night. So it's terrific, right? So I'm in heaven.

(Arnold Schwarzenegger in "Pumping Iron")

The classic documentary on bodybuilding was released in 1977 and that was about the time I read the article on Casey Viator, the teenage Mr. America. I think it's easy to understand why I was fascinated with bodybuilding. The combination of sex and muscles should be appealing to every young man . . . and, hopefully, a lot of beautiful young women. And nobody has articulated it as graphically or as humorously as Arnold. It's still one of my favorite movie scenes and has hundreds of thousands of hits on YouTube.

When I got to Cherry Point, North Carolina, my permanent duty station in the Marines, I was 18 years old and I quickly found that they had a great gym. For the next three and a half years, I was a fixture. I was 165 pounds when I got into the Marines and two years later, I weighed 220 and it was all muscle. When I took a leave, I went to stay with the Steins and visited my high school. I ran into my football coach and he was shocked.

"Where the hell was this when you were here? *Now* you're a man. Great."

The gym became my salvation in the military and it's served that same purpose since then. I still spend way too much time in the gym and when I have had the opportunity to meet and speak to Arnold on a couple of occasions I thanked him for ruining my life by giving me a lifelong obsession. That at least made him laugh.

Bodybuilding is responsible for me finding yoga and I had the same first impression: I was hooked. I immediately liked the physical aspects of yoga – the stretching and the calisthenics. Just those parts make you feel good. If you go to a physical trainer and he stretches you out, you're going to feel better.

In yoga, you add the philosophy and everything else that we teach – like connecting your breath to the movement, contracting the muscles on the exhale, expanding the muscles on the inhale and meditation – and it just makes you feel fantastic. I had that feeling after the first class I took 20 years ago and I still feel it today. Every time I leave a yoga class, I feel fucking great.

* * *

What separates me from conventional yoga teachers is that I place yoga and weight training on equal ground. I would suffer without either of them. I have a unique background unlike any other yogi that I've met – 35 years of elite level weight training experience, 20 years of yoga practice with 15 of those spent as a top tier teacher. I don't think anyone teaching today has been combining those two skills that long and is qualified to teach both as well as I am.

I would not, however, combine my yoga practice with my strength and conditioning sessions, not only for many complex physiological reasons, but also because I like to separate my churches. My yoga is the temple to my humanity and my weight training is the church of my vanity. As I get older their differences are shrinking.

But the approach to teaching each of them is exactly the same. Most yoga teachers think that yoga is all you need and that weight training is violent on the body. But I believe to maximize your health, you need it all. When I discovered yoga, I transferred the way it was taught to the way I worked with weights and to me, they are exactly the same. I think if you approach conditioning and strength training in the same way with the same mentality that you do yoga, it is healing and healthy and not damaging.

There are three pillars you need to practice to improve your body – strength, flexibility and cardiovascular conditioning. Yogis who try to protect their brand say you can get all three in yoga, but that's not true. If you want to build muscles, you have to progressively overload them. If you want to strengthen your legs, you put barbells on your shoulders and do squats. There is no equivalent of that in yoga. None.

I had a woman in a recent class of mine and she is a world renowned yogi. But if you look at her, she's out of shape. She's happy, so that's great. If people are fulfilled and happy and overweight I don't care. But if they want to change their body, yoga isn't going to do that. It may change it to a degree because all of a sudden you become conscious about what you eat and you don't eat too many doughnuts.

Yoga preaches non-violence, which leads some people to abstain from meat because of the way animals are killed. After those people become vegans, they start to lose weight but they don't change their body composition. I call it skinny fat. They're skinny, but they're still soft. Like supermodels. They have no muscle tone but they look pretty good until you really look at them. The powerful thing about yoga is finding your union and how it brings you to your center. But you can find that in strength training, too. And in strength training, you can find yoga.

* * *

A lot of people think weight training is boring and they don't want to do it. But I tell them it's not what you're doing; it's how you're doing it. That is where I have found similarities between teaching yoga and strength training. I think yoga technique applies to each because building the body is spiritual and physical. So when you are training, can you be connected with what you're doing? Can you feel what you're doing? Can you use your focus, awareness, your consciousness? Can you use imagination, visualization and manifest the kind of life you want, the kind of health you want, the kind of relationship you want, the kind of job you want?

That's what freeing your mind is. Your mind will get you on the same patterns of defeat, the same patterns of distraction, the same patterns of failure. But you have to find a technique to rise above those things. Like any athlete, you have to figure out a way to overcome them. So it's not what you do – it can be running or weight training or writing or knitting – you have to focus on freeing your mind. I think that's why people like to knit – because it's so meditative. You're just focused on that one thing. It's repetition. Yoga is about repetition. Repetition creates freedom. How does it do that? You're doing the same thing over and over again until you become skilled at it. It's like a guy playing golf and he's practicing with the putter and he's got 50 balls he's going to putt. He's free of any thought at that moment.

In the movie *The Legend of Bagger Vance*, there's a great scene where Bobby Jones, who was the best golfer in the world in the 1920s, looks down the fairway and the fairway collapses. He becomes so focused that he drowns out the noise and hits the ball to that small area that only he can see. Everything becomes silent. That's the way it was for Michael Jordan playing basketball. There was one time during a game when Jordan closed his eyes while shooting a free throw and still made it. He was taunting the other team at the time, but he could make it because he was free and focused. That's what yoga is. It's not what you're doing, it's how you're doing it. You're completely involved in what I call the five doors – focus, awareness, consciousness, imagination, and visualization. And if you can grasp those five things and put them together, man you're right there.

As outrageous and funny as it was, Arnold Schwarzenegger was scientifically onto something in his description of the pump because he was describing the mind and body connection. That is what is powerful about yoga. Connecting the mind to what you're doing. Focus on the muscle. Use the imagination like you feel you're using every muscle strand. I can walk in to a yoga class and be in a mental mess. I can walk in lethargic. I can walk in and my body hurts all over. But I walk out a 180 in all three areas because I just spent an hour and a half in focusing on very simple movements, nothing contorted, my mind free. I pour out a bucket of sweat. I ease my mind with meditation and I walk out feeling amazing.

And for me, the same is true with weight training because of the way I approach it and utilize yoga techniques. I leave the gym and I feel awesome. I'm not sure I have quite the same feeling expressed by Arnold, but I feel pretty good.

CHAPTER 13 - DISCOVERING THE JOYS OF SILENCE

Although full enlightenment was indeed a journey down a jagged road, I think enlightenment has been within me in some form my entire life. That may seem contradictory for someone who found punching another human being to be a joyous exercise, but I've never denied the anger I had from losing both parents, particularly my mother.

Yet I look back and remember times when I went out of my way to find a peaceful feeling. When I was living with the Pughs on the pig farm, I would go into the woods by myself, just to get away from everyone. My anger issues were extreme at the time - killing birds for the fun of it is a good example. But away from everyone, I found tranquility. Without knowing it, I had discovered a very primitive form of meditation.

Ten years ago, I discovered the real thing when I went to a meditation retreat at the California Vipassana Center in North Fork, which is near Yosemite National Park. The teacher was S.N. Goenka, one of the most famous teachers of meditation in the world. He was considered one of the masters of *Vipassana* meditation and I had a profound experience.

The retreat lasted 10 days and while you know it is going to be a unique experience, nothing can prepare you for how strict the rules are going be. As soon as you step on the property, you can't make eye contact with anyone. There's no talking, no cell phones, no prayer, no yoga, no exercise. There's one thing: Sitting there and meditating. And they teach you from scratch how to do it.

There were about 100 people in the class with the men on one side of the room and women on the other. Men were housed at one end of the property and the women were at the opposite end. We got up every day at 4:30 a.m. and would immediately go to the room, where no one said anything. We would meditate until 8 a.m., then stop for breakfast.

We came back and meditated from about 10 a.m. to 2 p.m. and stopped for lunch. We resumed meditating after lunch and went until about 7 p.m. In all, it was about 12 hours of meditation a day.

The first three days are rugged. You basically go insane because you've turned off all stimuli, except your own mind. They sit you down and teach you a technical way of doing it. They show a short video of Goenka on TV and he says, "You have 10 days to practice seriously, to practice diligently, to practice consistently," and then he goes into his discourse and he talks for maybe a half hour. After that, he tells you to close your eyes and he starts his meditation.

At the end of the day, there is a second course and then you go home and go to bed and you start again the next day. You do that 10 days in a row – no eye contact, no phones, no nothing. So it drives you crazy for awhile. But then about the fifth or sixth day, you get really solid. All of a sudden you're sitting there not moving for like five hours at a time after the first three days when you were fidgeting like hell. You have to get still in your mind because if you don't the body goes crazy. And vice versa. You've got to get the body still in order to still the mind and you've got to get the mind still in order to still the body.

Goenka compared sensations you experience in everyday life to a bubble that increases to a certain size and then pops and fades away. His point was to focus on your own well-being and not get distracted by minor irritations, which was a big lesson for me. I had spent much of my adult life beating the hell out of people because of minor irritations.

Like the bubble that pops and goes away, so do small frustrations. Why do you become attached to something that is not permanent? Why are you mad in traffic when traffic is only three minutes long? If it is not permanent, there is no reason to be upset about it.

So I use that philosophy when I teach yoga. I put students in a pose and they say they're dying. I say can you not live with it for 30 seconds? Won't you be better for it? Even if it hurts for three minutes, can you not be still for three minutes? Can you not be unattached to the pain that you're feeling? You're not going to get hurt, it's just discomfort. Can you be calm and centered in this moment?

Although they urge you to go back to the meditation center once a year, I've never been back. The first time lasts 10 days, but the second is only three days because you've been initiated and you understand how to meditate. I never have been back because I was always working and just couldn't take the time off to go. But what I learned at the center has made meditation part of my daily life and as Goenka said, if you don't understand meditation, you can't learn yoga.

I think meditation plays a huge role in the health benefits of yoga. I read a study recently that yoga can reduce your health costs by 43 percent. There are now a lot of military people doing yoga because it is a great way to relieve stress and anxiety. I wish I had known about it when I was nine years old. I would have recommended it for my brother Freddy, who had PTSD and could have used it. Of course, at the time, I don't think he would have taken my suggestion.

But one of the many great gifts yoga has provided me is an overpowering sense of calm. When I think back to those early turbulent days after my mother died, I am at peace. I don't hold grudges because I have learned that a grudge is like Goenka's bubble. It fades away so there's no reason to hold on to it.

CHAPTER 14 - THE ROSE OF MY LIFE

People who have experienced everything from great success to devastating adversity have many clichés they can use to describe their lives – ups and downs, highs and lows, peaks and valleys and so on.

In my case, life has been more like a visit to the carnival. I've had fast rides, scary rides, played real life games of chance and skill, observed and been a part of many sideshows and met my share of hot dogs. I've even cleaned up after the animals.

I don't have many warm memories of my childhood. After my mother died, I did not grow up with parents or siblings. I was raised by strangers; surrounded by people but alone in life. I was never able to brag or ever talk about "my family." The Pughs, Steins and others were kind and I'm grateful they all gave me a safe place to sleep and food to eat. But I knew I was always a visitor, not blood, not family.

Those who were fortunate enough to come from stable backgrounds have a strong sense of family as they get older. For many years, I did not have that. Then I found yoga. I didn't know it at the time, but yoga and the yoga community became my family.

And then along came a Rose.

When I was 50, I was seeing a woman named Kimberly. We'd been dating for about five months and I don't think either of us felt the relationship was going to change our lives.

We were wrong. One night, I was watching the series finale of

24, one of my all-time favorite shows. Jack Bauer, the featured character, was the ultimate badass, constantly beating the hell out of people to save the world. He reminded me of my days as a cop in the afternoon and bouncer in the evening, trying to keep the peace while kicking ass at the same time. During the show, Kim called and said, "I think I'm pregnant." I kind of thought "Yeah, sure," and hung up quickly so I could continue watching Jack. Kim is really an amazing person, but she has a tendency to be a bit dramatic and sometimes fears the worse so I wasn't that concerned by the call.

But then, Kim took a pregnancy test and, well, a woman knows her body. She was, in fact, pregnant. At age 50, I was going to become a father. Once again, I was behind, a "late bloomer" in every sense of the term.

Scarlett Rose Smith – a flowery, melodic name I think my mother would love – was born on October 11, 2010. Reality and true adulthood set in for me damn near overnight. I had to get my shit together because life was no longer about me alone. I had to get life insurance, start a college fund and create a savings account for the baby. To top it all off, Kim and I did not remain together as a couple. Hell, I mean, what were the chances? We barely had time to get to know each other before the child came and the panic set in.

The real strength of our relationship, however, was friendship. And to this day, nearly six years later, we are former lovers and best of friends – kind of like Jerry and Elaine on *Seinfeld*.

Kim, like most moms, does most of the heavy lifting when it comes to caring for Scarlett. I'm the hunter. Kim also did not come from a stable family so between the two of us, we didn't have a clue how difficult having a child would be.

But you figure it out. We both work hard as parents and Scarlett is a delight – beautiful, brilliant, thriving and happy. As for Kimberly, she could not be a more devoted or caring mother. It's a joy for me to watch a mother and child bond. Through them, I have a better understanding of what I lost when my mother died. I will always be grateful to Kimberly, who gave me the gift of family. I know that I will always have her back and she will have mine.

* * *

Scarlett, of course, is the most important member of my family, but I also have a sister and a half-brother. My brother was not successful as a 21-year-old surrogate parent and I did not see my sister and I had separate lives. But they are still family, all of us from the same living mother.

So when I go back to North Carolina, I visit them. I don't go often, but as I grew older, I wanted to connect with my roots. Since Freddy, my half-brother, was 12 years older than me, he was able to tell me stories about my mother and father. I also met Freddy's dad and he told me all about meeting and marrying my mother. I was so moved when he told me the story of how they had received a waiver from the Vatican, which allowed a non-Catholic to be married in the church, that I went to Italy to see the church. That was important to me – another way of connecting with my past. I even tried to find some of my mother's relatives, but had no luck.

Although my sister Chris and I always lived in the Greensboro area, after we were separated I didn't see her for 10 years. After I moved to L.A., we had no communication. She had a very different life than me. After my mom died, Chris and I went to the foster home owned by the single mom named Laura. I apparently was acting out my confusion and anger, so I was shipped out but Chris stayed. Laura was the only foster parent Chris had. She lived there until she was old enough to move out, but she and Laura remained close friends and Laura is still a second mother to her.

Chris' early life was far more stable than mine, although she missed out on some truly unique experiences. For example, she never had a pet pig named Pug.

I'm sure she has more pleasant childhood memories than me, but her adult life has not been great. She has been divorced, has a teenage kid and sometimes was in such a bind for money that she had to live with Freddy to share expenses. The farthest she ventured away from Greensboro was to go to college at Appalachian State, which is about 100 miles away. When I found out what her life had been like, I thought, "Holy shit. That could have been me." If I had stayed with Laura, I probably would be in the restaurant business in North Carolina and I doubt I would have ever discovered yoga.

Despite the past and whatever differences we have, Freddy and Chris are family and important to me. But when we do see each other, it is always me finding them. When I wanted to find them at

30, I found them. At 40, I found them. Same thing at 50. That, I'm sure, is part of my yearning for that family connection.

Freddy would have had to have been very special to be a successful 21-year-old parent to kids 12 and nine. But he had been in action as a gunner in Vietnam and he was crazy as hell. I came to realize that when he roughed me up, it was because he knew no better. So any resentment I had towards him disappeared long ago.

When my brother, sister and I meet, we hug but they are not nearly as emotional or huggy as I am. I've always tried to rise above any bad feelings I might have about them because they are family and I never had enough of that as a kid. I'm not going to reject it now because they're not like I am, or not like I might want them to be. I've freed myself from that. It's always been me surviving on my own, my own skills, my own motivation and I embrace that.

One thing I have mastered is the art of forgiveness. I'll hold a grudge for a minute, but if someone makes amends to me, even in the smallest way, and takes one step towards me, I'll take twenty steps towards them and resolve the situation. To me, part of the philosophical aspect of yoga is forgiveness – not so much for people who act like jerks. Screw them. But it's for me. I want to be able to relax and not sit around mumbling to myself "I'd like to kill this motherfucker."

* * *

When I do go to North Carolina, I always drive by our old house.

One time, there was a man in the backyard so I stopped and talked to him. It turned out that he bought the house after we moved out in 1970, but he said it was from someone else. Apparently my mother had rented it, something I never knew.

Despite being only nine years old when I moved out, I had vivid memories of several things in the house. I asked him if at the back of the house was there was a cement patio with tiny handprints, he said there was. We went to look at it and I said, “Those are mine.” He goes, “You’re kidding me.” It was a very emotional moment for me. If I had been a musician, I would have written a song about it. I’ll never forget the sight of those little handprints made by an innocent boy whose stable life was to last only a year or two longer.

After seeing the handprints, I wanted to see more. So I asked the man if there was still a circular light in the kitchen ceiling. He said there was not and that maybe I was thinking about another house. But he offered to go inside and take a look. So we went into the kitchen and he pointed at the ceiling and said, “See, there’s nothing circular.” But I told him to look closer. You could see a slight indentation under the paint and it was circular. He was amazed that I had that memory from 40 years earlier. I realized later that he had doubted me – even after seeing my handprints.

When I left, I realized that part of me had wanted to reclaim the house, which should have been mine. There was always that part of me that never wanted to leave. And that was the only place where I had known my mother.

A few years later, the man called me and offered to sell the house to me, but it wasn't practical to own it while living 3,000 miles away. And even though the house had some special memories for me, it also had some painful ones. Owning it would have been a huge gamble – a one-way ticket either to depression or liberation. It was too close to call and I had no desire to take a chance. And maybe that's another benefit of having Scarlett so late in life. She is my future. The past, especially mine, is better left in the past.

CHAPTER 15 - YOU CAN RUN BUT YOU CAN'T HIDE

As I have noted a few times, a constant theme in my life has been doing something late. I told my yoga class that I have always been 10 years behind where I should be. I had my first child at 50, but it should have been 40, I graduated high school at 28, and it should have been 18.

When I say that, it goes right over their heads. So I have to tell them – it's a joke. I finished high school on time, but I've been late for everything else.

Which recently turned out to work in my favor.

For many years, I thought I wouldn't live very long. My mom died of an aneurysm at 42 and my dad died of a heart defect at 33. When you have genes like that, you figure by the time retirement comes around, you won't be around.

On the other hand, maybe fear of an early death is what motivated me to be so active in my life. Since I went into the Marines at 18 years old, I have been a workout warrior. I still spend many hours in the gym in addition to many hours practicing and teaching yoga. I am 56 years old, but I do not take any sort of medication, except, occasionally, Advil for sore muscles. My blood pressure is a constant 115/75 and although I am bulky because of weight lifting, I am relatively lean.

Overall, I feel amazing.

Or at least I did until the spring of 2016 when I found out, again, that nothing is guaranteed in life.

I was at the end of an hour-long workout lifting weights when I felt a burning sensation in my chest. A few weeks before I had a really bad cold so I thought the chest pain might be a respiratory infection. I decided to take three days off with no exercise and see if I could get the problem cleared up.

I felt better after the rest and went for a bike ride, but felt the pain again. So I took another day off.

The next day, however, I was driving in traffic when I felt it again and it scared the hell out of me. Still, because of where the pain was in my chest, I thought it was respiratory and not related to the heart. I get health care through the Veteran's Administration, but they have a long waiting time and a doctor could not see me for about six weeks. By the time I made the appointment, however, the pain had gone away so I thought everything was okay.

For several days, I was fine. But one morning after I got up, I felt a tightness in my chest. I thought about going to the hospital, but I had a long workday scheduled, so I rested for 10 minutes or so to see if the tightness would go away, and it did. I put in 12 hours of work, but at the end of the day, I decided there had been too many incidents to ignore and I needed to see a doctor. So I checked into a hospital.

When they first examined me, they couldn't find anything, but because of my family history, they wanted me to stay overnight until a cardiologist could see me. When he did, he discovered that the main artery was 95 percent blocked.

I was stunned. I had already lived 24 years longer than my

father and 15 years longer than my mother, so this was one time that being late worked in my favor. But that was small consolation. My father had been taken down by heart problems and there I was – in the hospital with a heart problem. The irony was I had done everything I could to run away from my family history. I moved across the country, away from the pain of losing my parents early in life. I was a fitness fanatic who, yes, had a few vices along the way. But those were for very short periods and even when I was hanging around with a drug dealer, I still was spending serious time in the gym.

I had run hard and far to get away from my family history. Hell, I'd even changed my name! But all I could do was shake my head, curse the irony and realize that another cliché had been proven to be true in my life: You can run, but you can't hide.

My family history had caught up with me.

* * *

I was scheduled for an angioplasty on a Tuesday and I was not looking forward to having a heart attack. And what is a "mild" heart attack, anyway? Isn't that like being a "little" pregnant? An angioplasty is not considered surgery, so the patient stays awake. I knew that despite medication, it was going to hurt like hell.

I would have preferred to be asleep not only for the procedure, but also for the preparation. I knew it was not going to be a good experience when I found myself of an operating table, butt-naked with a catheter in my penis and six nurses surrounding me. Female nurses. They were pros, of course, and were used to that situation I'm sure. But I wasn't. It was so uncomfortable that I finally gave into the absurdity of it all and said to the nurses, "Who brought the wine and baby oil?" Somehow, I found my sense of humor and they laughed.

The heart attack didn't feel worth a damn, but the good news is that the procedure fixed everything. After resting a few days, I felt great, resumed my workouts and began teaching my yoga classes again. I also got to celebrate my good fortune, and that came in the form of my daughter. Although I have outlived both of my parents, the fact is if my heart problem had been like my dad's and been fatal, I would have left Scarlett at age five.

The thought of that is horrible. Fortunately over the years, I have met many great people and developed great relationships. Barry Turner and Dr. Chris Gronet are fabulously successful people. When I found out what was happening with my heart, I texted both of them and asked for a couple of favors. If I died, could they make sure Kim was able to move to the East Coast where her family lives? And would they take care of my daughter?

Both said hell yeah. Don't worry. We will make sure she has everything she needs. College will be paid for. But let's make sure that's not going to happen.

Obviously I'm glad it didn't and that unlike my parents, I'll be around as Scarlett goes through life. Although it was surprising to have a kid at my age, her life gave me new life at the time, and that continues. I had a friend who's the same age as I am but never had a kid. He had an interesting take on life when I told him my girlfriend was pregnant with Scarlett. "That's pretty optimistic of you," he said because I was a 50-year-old guy and it's a young man's game. By the time she's ready to go to college, I'll be retirement age.

But I think I've got a lot of hustle left in me. I'm 56 so I can hustle maybe 10 or 15 more years and will be able to take care of my daughter's needs. I had her at an age where many parents are becoming grandparents, but I think - depending, of course, how young she might be when she has her first kid - that I have a chance to know my grandchildren.

Although the heart problem was scary, now that it has been taken care of, I have continued being optimistic about the future. I have done some research on my family history and discovered that an Irishman named John Woods was the founding father of our family. He lived from 1720 to 1820, which is an amazing long life even today. In that era, many men did not live past 40 and to get to 50 was the exception, not the rule. Neither of my parents made it to their 43rd birthday, but John Woods was 100 years old when he died. I think I have his genes.

I'm also confident that yoga will extend my life. I know it already has. Without it, maybe I would have had this problem earlier in life. Without yoga, maybe my body and mind would not have been strong enough to overcome the family genes that took my parents' lives. For me and many others, there is something very powerful about yoga. Look what it's done for me. It's made me at peace with my past, freed my mind from the pain of losing parents before age 10, wiped out the anger of a brutal childhood, banished the shitbird mentality that thought shooting phone booths on a military base with an M-16 or a champagne bottle with a 9 mm pistol on a rooftop in Beverly Hills was normal, made the thrill of fighting and beating people up disappear and turned a boy who was irresponsible and lost into a man – an optimistic man planning a very long life.

CHAPTER 16 - IT'S NOT OVER 'TILL IT'S OVER

The night before I began writing this final chapter, my beloved North Carolina Tar Heels suffered a devastating loss in the 2016 NCAA basketball championship game to Villanova. The disaster unfolded in the most dramatic and heartbreaking fashion - a game-winning shot by Villanova as time expired. Actually, I'm being too kind. It was not a shot. It was a prayer, heaved up from 27 feet.

At that moment, I just stood there, silent and in disbelief. Only seconds earlier, I had felt elation. With less than five minutes left in the game, the Tar Heels were 10 points behind, but they never seemed rattled. They kept chipping away at the lead and after an amazing three-point shot by guard Marcus Paige with 4.7 seconds left, the score was tied at 74.

Over the years, I had witnessed excellence by my Tar Heels, who are one of the most successful college basketball programs. Only five colleges have at least five national championships - UCLA has 11, Kentucky has eight and North Carolina, Duke and Indiana each have five. I have also witnessed miracles - some of you surely remember a freshman named Michael Jordan making a game-winning shot in the 1982 NCAA title game. So I had faith that our tradition and pedigree would be too much for the Wildcats. We had them right where we wanted them - reeling from our comeback and knowing our great history.

But not this time. A confident kid named Kris Jenkins ignored how far he was from the basket, let the ball go with less than a second left, and when it went through the hoop, there were zeros on the clock and Villanova had a 77-74 victory.

When I did finally sit down to write, the loss was still on my mind, but so was the bigger picture. Sports are about more than just playing games. You learn how to win, but you also have to learn about losing because life is inevitably full of losses.

More importantly, however, sports teach you how to keep fighting. Life is a standing-room-only, sold-out, heavyweight championship fight and the goal is to put in the necessary work to be in a position to win at the buzzer if necessary, but preferably a lot sooner.

* * *

Although I have had colorful experiences, my goal in writing this book has always been to understand and explain the bigger picture in life. As I struggled putting that into words, I watched Carolina lose to Villanova and I was reminded of my own defeats and triumphs. From all of them, I got something positive. It did not always happen right away, but that was the end result. My hope is that my story illustrates how all of us can transcend our birth circumstance, our mistakes and our fears to become something greater.

I started watching Carolina games nearly 50 years ago with my mother and because she happened to own a restaurant where legendary coach Dean Smith ate, I adopted him as a role model and watched him closely over the years. We did not have a personal relationship, but I felt mentored by him by proxy.

There were others who became men of profound influence to a fatherless boy - C.K. Siler, my high school football coach, my Marine drill instructors and some of those 1980s action movie heroes, who always did the right thing.

But even though those positive role models had great success, I also learned they had to handle failure or disappointment. Dean Smith coached Carolina for 36 years but won only two championships. So he lost the final game of the season 34 times.

And as great as North Carolina has been, the NCAA tournament is 78 years old. Winning five titles is more impressive than the majority of programs, but they have not won the tournament 73 times.

The message is no one is entitled. Success must be earned and earned daily. Yes, there are days when you feel beaten down and all is lost. Go ahead, allow yourself a day at most to wallow in your self-pity, then get your ass back up and come back fighting. When you think about it logically, what's the alternative?

Competing in athletics, watching sports, being in the military, becoming a fanatic weight lifter and workout warrior and mastering yoga have taught me discipline and dedication. I've learned how to navigate life. The traits I developed and the experiences I've had afforded me hope when there was none. In many instances, those experiences have even saved my ass when life seemed to have crumbled and I neared desperation.

The routines I have established in life have enabled me to walk by faith and not by sight. They have given me strength to overcome many obstacles and have helped place my feet and mind on solid ground. They have taken the place of family and mentors. When no one else provided direction, they were the positive influence in my life.

* * *

Tomorrow and Mondays are my favorite days. Why? Because no matter what happens today, tomorrow begins with a clean slate. I consider Mondays the beginning of a seven-day, seven-game series. Just once I'd like to end the week undefeated, going 7-0 and doing everything perfectly the way I planned it. Most weeks, if I'm honest with myself, I usually end up 4-3 or maybe 5-2. But I'm tough on myself and everyone should be. If you are 7-0 on Sunday evening, you may want to up the ante for the next week. Maybe you're playing it safe, but to move forward, you have to play at the edge.

After a win, a great coach may say, "We were very fortunate today, we got some breaks and some things went our way, but we're not where we want to be. I'm going to enjoy this win for awhile, but we have a lot of work to do to get better."

After a defeat, the same coach may say, "We will use this disappointment as motivation to work harder. That's what life is all about. I told my team that this loss does not define us. What defines us is how we respond."

That's my blueprint for life. My dad died when I was an infant. I never had a man other than my coaches or military officers teach me how to win or how to handle losing in life. The few lessons I received were impersonal, never delivered in a one-on-one setting. In those group situations, I would listen, absorb and try to apply what small lesson I had learned to my life. But truthfully, I always learned the hard way. And that's okay because I have found that to be the most efficient and longest lasting way.

Looking back at the day Freddy, my half-brother, brought my sister and me into the living room to tell us mother had died was the starting point of my purification. The explosion of that moment raged in me for a long time and there was no one to help me deal with it. The families I lived with gave me a bed, food and clothes, but they did not give me direction or love. Over the years, I came to the realization that the anger I felt from my youth was either going to consume me or I would somehow overcome it and be motivated by it. And I succeeded in the latter.

When Chris, my sister, fell to the floor in despair at our mother's death, I sat there, stoic and still. I must have known that I had to become a boy warrior because my childhood had instantly become much more difficult, challenging and lonely. Fate demanded that I change quickly. The trauma of my mother dying, Freddy's abuse, being separated from my sister and the frightening uncertainty not only of the future, but also of the next day simply made me tougher at an early age. Looking back, the resilience I developed as an adult was the result of the horror of my childhood.

But, as I have said, believe it or not, I would not change a thing. It would have been nice for the road to have been a little less jagged with far fewer potholes, but if you are happy with who you are, you recognize that the end is a result of the journey.

I believe you gain wisdom from the past and the lessons you learn help you from making the same mistakes over and again. But other than the cathartic exercise of writing this book, I've found that it's best if I don't invest too much time thinking about the past. Looking back generally leads to regret for mistakes you made or good choices you did not make. That is maddening and is a waste of time.

Ultimately, the only direction you should look is straight ahead. There are no guarantees in life and some dreams turn into nothing more than fantasies. But if you are able to live in the moment and prepare for the future, you'll see that life is full of opportunities. For me, that's finding enlightenment.

But if you are able to live in the moment and prepare for the future, you'll see that life is so god damn full of opportunities, only never give up and never stop looking for them, they are there, that's yoga and that's life. For me, Rudy Mettia, that's also finding enlightenment. Y'all breathing? Now go find yours!

Acknowledgements

This book would not be possible without the contributions of many beautiful souls, past and present. Thanks to Jan Hubbard, my co-writer, for organizing my thoughts, encouraging me to dig deep into memories that were often painful but sometimes funny and pleasant, polishing my words to remove any hint of Southern Redneck left in me after all these years and continually reminding me that you have one shot at an autobiography so make sure it is special.

Howie Baral, my tenacious producer, friend, and fellow yoga teacher can sometimes be a royal pain in the ass because he pushes me relentlessly. But he believes my story may help others transcend their own circumstances so they can create a brighter future for themselves, and I am flattered and honored by that. Howie has encouraged me to write this book for several years and without his backing and drive, the project would have never gotten off the ground. I am grateful for his generosity and his belief in me.

Yariv Lerner, founder of Udaya Entertainment, is a dear friend, mentor and great influence in my life as well as countless others. He pulled me from obscurity and has never said "no" to me once, no matter how outrageous the request, and has always believed in me against all logic. His support has been invaluable and I will fight to the end with him and for him.

Thanks to the very gifted Englishman Andrew Hannon, not only for his creativity, knowledge and meticulous copy editing, but also for publishing this book.

I never knew my father, Rudy David Smith, who died when I was an infant, but Dad – thanks for bringing me into this world.

To my mother Vera: Nine years was far too few with you but you've had a lasting impact on my life. It's been almost 50 years since we've been together, but the love I have for you is as powerful as it was the day you were taken from me. I take comfort in knowing that I am only a single heartbeat or breath away from seeing you again.

To Kimberly, the mother of my daughter, thank you for the gift of our daughter. Words cannot express the joy you have brought me in Scarlett Rose Smith, the centerpiece of my life. You have been a rock and a wonderful role model for our daughter. The motherly love that you shower her with on a daily basis is inspirational and will help shape her for the rest of her life. Thank you for being kind and supportive of me when walking, no, running away might have been the wiser choice. I thank you very much and I promise – I have your back now and always.

To Jennifer, thank you for loving me unconditionally. It is a blessing that many are never fortunate enough to experience. You have stuck by me through thick and thin. You are family and Scarlett and I both love you.

To my extended family who have helped me at one time or another on this, well, unusual journey – my longtime best friends, brothers, and sisters in life, Barry Turner, Dr. Chris Gronet, Dimitris Christoforidis, Craig Thigpen, Chris Taggert, Holly Butler, Patty Van de Bogart and the rest of our Udaya tribe – you guys are simply the best. To my brother Freddy, and my sister Caresse, thank you for not rescuing me; you had your own struggles and burdens to bear and had I been found I would not have had the blessing of going through this life's learning experiences from which this book was harvested.

To my fellow yoga teachers light warriors who I have practiced with over the years and learned so much from that most can be known just by their first name, Annie, John, Maty, Lisa, Baron, Vinnie, Jerome, Seane, and many others. To the hundreds of thousands of students who I've had the privilege to teach over these past many years, thanks for your trust, your kindness, attention, devotion and support. I've learned more from you than you could ever know and I hope to see you on the mat for many years forward, God willing.

To all the foster families that took me in, from that young, lost and helpless boy, thank you. We were meant to meet if only for an instance and I trust that you know you were appreciated and doing God's work by taking in the abandoned.

Finally, I must acknowledge the rebel and the visionary, Bryan Kest. You lead from example and I'm indebted to you for the life I have now. Without you crossing my path and bringing yoga down from the clouds to where I could understand and apply it to my life, this book would tell a very different story. You have been a very important influence in my life and I will be forever grateful for the way you have believed in me and shown me the way, more often than not, by your actions, not words.

Made in the USA
Las Vegas, NV
15 December 2023

82860029R00115